Janelle Monáe's Queer Afrofuturism

Global Media and Race

Series Editor: Frederick Luis Aldama, The Ohio State University

Global Media and Race is a series focused on scholarly books that examine race and global media culture. Titles focus on constructions of race in media, including digital platforms, webisodes, multilingual media, mobile media, vlogs, and other social media, film, radio, and television. The series considers how race—and intersectional identities generally—is constructed in front of the camera and behind, attending to issues of representation and consumption as well as the making of racialized and anti-racist media phenomena from script to production and policy.

Dan Hassler-Forest, *Janelle Monáe's Queer Afrofuturism: Defying Every Label*
Patricia Saldarriaga and Emy Manini, *Infected Empires: Decolonizing Zombies*
Bronwyn Carlson and Jeff Berglund, eds., *Indigenous Peoples Rise Up: The Global Ascendency of Social Media Activism*
Matthew David Goodwin, *The Latinx Files: Race, Migration, and Space Aliens*
Hyesu Park, ed., *Media Culture in Transnational Asia: Convergences and Divergences*
Melissa Castillo Planas, *A Mexican State of Mind: New York City and the New Borderlands of Culture*
Monica Hanna and Rebecca A. Sheehan, eds., *Border Cinema: Reimagining Identity through Aesthetics*

Janelle Monáe's Queer Afrofuturism

■■■■■■■■■■■■■■■■■■■■■■■■■■■■

Defying Every Label

DAN HASSLER-FOREST

Rutgers University Press

New Brunswick, Camden, and Newark, New Jersey, and London

Library of Congress Cataloging-in-Publication Data

Names: Hassler-Forest, Dan, author.
Title: Janelle Monáe's queer afrofuturism : defying every label / Dan Hassler-Forest.
Description: New Brunswick : Rutgers University Press, 2022. |
  Series: Global media and race | Includes bibliographical references and index.
Identifiers: LCCN 2021039240 | ISBN 9781978826687 (paperback) |
  ISBN 9781978826694 (hardback) | ISBN 9781978826700 (epub) |
  ISBN 9781978826717 (mobi) | ISBN 9781978826724 (pdf)
Subjects: LCSH: Monáe, Janelle—Criticism and interpretation. | Popular music—
  History and criticism. | Mass media and music. | Science fiction in music. |
  Afrofuturism. | Gender identity in music.
Classification: LCC ML420.M5582 H37 2022 | DDC 782.42164092—dc23
LC record available at https://lccn.loc.gov/2021039240

A British Cataloging-in-Publication record for this book is available from the British Library.

Song lyrics from "Evolution (and Flashback)" by Gil Scott-Heron reproduced with permission
from The Estate of Gil Scott-Heron and Brouhaha Music Inc.

References to internet websites (URLs) were accurate at the time of writing. Neither the author
nor Rutgers University Press is responsible for URLs that may have expired or changed since the
manuscript was prepared.

⊖ The paper used in this publication meets the requirements of the American National Standard
for Information Sciences—Permanence of Paper for Printed Library Materials, ANSI
Z39.48-1992.

www.rutgersuniversitypress.org

Manufactured in the United States of America

Contents

Janelle Monáe's Queer Afrofuturism

Introduction

■■■■■■■■■■■■■■■■■■■■■■■

Singer. Dancer. Movie star. Activist. Queer icon. Afrofuturist. Working class heroine. Time traveler. Prophet. Black radical. Fashionista. Feminist. Diva. Android. Dirty Computer.

Janelle Monáe is all of these things, and more. Her lyrics soar. Her music connects. Her film roles educate. Her outfits dazzle. Her speeches mobilize. Her emotion pictures sparkle. Her live shows tear the roof off. Her activism makes shit happen. And her pioneering work has inspired a generation of artists, musicians, filmmakers, performers, activists, and scholars.

It is difficult indeed to avoid hyperbole when describing Janelle Monáe. She has that rarest of star qualities that unites boundless talent with overpowering charisma, androgynous sex appeal, restless innovation, and that otherworldly manner we so easily associate with seers, mystics, and prophets. Prince and David Bowie had a similarly inspirational quality. Monáe shares not only their musical genius but also their ability to break down barriers of gender, sexuality, genre, and race. It has made her one of the most talked-about innovators in popular music. It has made her a celebrity whose creative output constantly supplements and enhances her activism. And it has made her the subject of this book.

For the uninitiated, Janelle Monáe is a Black[1] American writer, producer, and performer of popular music who has branched out into film, television, music production, and activism. She became known in the first place for her series of science fiction concept albums: *Metropolis: The Chase Suite* (2007)[2] was her major-label musical debut, a seven-track EP that offered a breath-less adventure narrative set in an elaborate future dystopia.[3] Her strikingly ambitious first full album *The ArchAndroid* (2010)[4] confirmed her prodigious talent as a singer, producer, and world-builder. The hit singles "Tight-rope" and "Cold War" brought her acclaim and visibility, while the concept album further elaborated her futuristic storyworld through her lyrics, soundscapes, and emotion pictures.[5] Three years later, *The Electric Lady* (2013)[6] cemented her reputation as a musical innovator, delivering a polished third concept album that added more new layers to her expanding storyworld.

At the same time, she kept short-circuiting her own fantastic world-building by creating constant slippages between future and present. Monáe strengthened this ambivalence by embracing two coexisting identities: she was both Cindi Mayweather, the twenty-eighth-century android character who had been declared an outlaw for falling in love with a human, and Janelle Monáe Robinson, a Black woman born on December 1, 1985, to working-class parents in Kansas City, Kansas. By intertwining these two realities across these three albums, Monáe created porous boundaries between her science-fictional storyworld and our own reality: the two constantly bleed into each other, just as her media appearances and social activism exist in dialogue with her creative work.

This sense of destabilization took a further turn with the release of her fourth album, *Dirty Computer*, in 2018.[7] The first three singles—"Django Jane," "Make Me Feel," and "PYNK"—departed from her established image: no tux, no tightly coiffed pompadour, no androids, no mention of Cindi Mayweather. These initial tracks and their videos combined an explicitly queer sexuality with a more fluid pop persona that seemed far removed from her previous android role-playing. But the forty-eight-minute emotion picture that accompanied the full album's release showed that she hadn't abandoned her love of science fiction: the narrative reframed the majority of the album's tracks as memories being erased from the mind of a prisoner in a chillingly dystopian near-future.

Meanwhile, Monáe also developed a successful career as a screen actor, lending her voice to the animated feature *Rio 2* (2014) before making her live-action acting debut in the history-making Black queer Oscar winner *Moonlight* (2016). That same year, she also played one of the leading roles in *Hidden Figures*, the dramatized history of three Black women whose work as mathematicians and engineers was instrumental to NASA's space program. Taking a leading role as an android in the first season of anthology series *Electric Dreams*, Monáe further reinforced her persona's association with science fiction.[8] Since then, she has continued to perform in screen roles, always in films that foreground social issues that are central to her work as an artist.

A third path in Monáe's career has been her commitment to activism. As her celebrity grew, she has increasingly used her platform to amplify the voices of social justice movements. She has spoken and performed at many protests and marches, has given rousing speeches at awards ceremonies and media debates, and has used her presence on social media to advance feminist, antiracist, and LGTBQ causes.

Taken together, these three interwoven strands form a multifaceted celebrity persona. More than merely a didactic vessel for political and ideological messaging, her work has questioned, challenged, and transformed ideas about race, gender, and sexuality. This dialogic approach is what holds together the many media, genres, platforms, and public roles she continues to navigate, and is therefore ultimately what makes her such a vitally important figure within global media culture.

This media culture has changed dramatically in the new millennium. In the twenty-first century, our media landscape has been increasingly dominated by the ongoing development of a variety of corporate-controlled multiplatform franchises.[9] But even though media production is increasingly monopolized by entertainment behemoths that translate easily to theme parks, LEGO play sets, T-shirts, Funko Pop figurines, and other forms of licensed merchandising,[10] artists and activists have also taken advantage of media convergence to use transmedia for their own ends.[11] For independent artists without a Disney-level production budget, this has helped them gain visibility while strengthening their message across a variety of media platforms.

In this book, I approach Janelle Monáe not only as the main creative force behind her self-authored world-building, but as a figure whose work brings together energies that unite creative production with social activism, interweaving them across different media platforms. Within this constellation of performances, characters, and narratives, a few specific energies have been consistent presences. These energies connect Monáe's transmedia work to a variety of different movements in art, theory, and politics. Rather than using a static term like "themes" or "topics," I see these energies as *vectors*: a term used in physics to describe "a quantity having direction as well as magnitude, especially as determining the position of one point in relation to another."[12] Similar terms have been used in philosophy and cultural theory, most notably in the work of Gilles Deleuze[13] and Alfred North Whitehead.[14]

I use the vector more pragmatically, as a straightforward concept that expresses the dynamic and immaterial forces of thought, creative work, and cultural power at play throughout Monáe's intricately networked oeuvre. It indicates the separate but complementary energies that work across and bind together our social, cultural, and political landscape. As movements that extend far beyond any individual artist's work, these vectors that run across Monáe's work expand the book's range: the concept emphasizes not only the intricate organization of her own creative output but also how it connects to larger networks of meaning.

These vectors help us visualize the deeper connections between popular culture and scholarship, while also acknowledging the creative text as theoretical exercise.[15] In Katherine McKittrick's words, "the practice of bringing together multiple texts, stories, songs, and place involves the difficult work of thinking and learning across many sites, and thus coming to know, generously, varying and shifting worlds and ideas."[16] My vectoral approach is an attempt to structure the theoretical dialogues her creative, performative, and activist work has helped to shape.

Five Vectors

This book's organization follows five such vectors: *Afrofuturism, Black feminism, intersectionality, posthumanism,* and *postcapitalism.* While these vectors identify the key energies that unite Monáe's work, they also extend outward toward other artists, movements, and theorists. The book's five chapters trace the ways in which these vectors provide a context, a network, and a playing field for the dynamic interaction between theory and creative practice. While the overall focus is primarily on Monáe's own output as a writer and producer, these vectors also trace the networked connections between her "core" works as a musician and actor (her own albums, videos, and screen performances) and more "peripheral" texts, such as film and television soundtracks to which she has contributed.

In this way, the book uses Janelle Monáe as a focal point through which we might reflect on the larger network of emergent and residual energies that bring together media, politics, and theory. These combined energies inform the social dynamics of culture, theory, and identity in twenty-first-century media culture, and the book's organization into five separate vectors illustrates how those interlocking energies have developed throughout Monáe's work. The first three chapters are focused primarily on her concept albums and emotion pictures, in roughly chronological order, while the last two more strongly foreground her contributions to other media. But each chapter also includes excursions to other artists and media texts that illustrate the many connections these vectors produce.

The first of these vectors situates Monáe's work within the larger cultural tradition of Afrofuturism: an ongoing creative project focused on "reimagining a future history of Blackness and technology."[17] As a Black utopian field, Afrofuturism provides radical visions of past, present, and future that remap our shared political horizons.[18] The chapter introduces the reader to the science fiction world-building that she has developed across her concept albums, in interviews and stage performances, and in her many emotion pictures. It illustrates the incremental development of Monáe's speculative storyworld, which simultaneously revives and reconfigures Afrofuturism as a transformative expression of the *dark fantastic*: her pathbreaking work as an Afrofuturist world-builder has contributed to the larger antiracist project of decolonizing our dreams and fantasies.[19]

The second chapter charts the vectoral movement of Black feminism across Monáe's work. Starting with a discussion of her starring role in the film *Hidden Figures* (2016), the chapter establishes Black feminism as a social, cultural, and political vector that ranges from popular mainstream expressions to more radical transformative work. The chapter relates this wide field of cultural expression to Black feminism's *dialectic of oppression and resistance*,[20] the dynamic that counters racial capitalism's *matrix of domination* with specific forms of activism as well as resistant creative work.[21] Where white liberal narratives have generally limited their focus to depictions of historical racism, Monáe's concept albums incorporate both sides of this dialectic in Cindi Mayweather's transformation from fugitive to rebel leader. The chapter therefore illustrates this dialectic with an analysis of expressions of Black feminism across Monáe's albums *The ArchAndroid* and *The Electric Lady*.

The third vector I identify throughout Monáe's work is that of intersectionality: a way of thinking and organizing based on the idea that social, cultural, and political power is constructed on the basis of complexly networked identities.[22] By foregrounding queerness as a destabilizing factor within these networks, intersectionality emphasizes the inherent multiplicity of individual identity, and expresses the fundamental relationality that underlies expressions of race, gender, and sexuality.[23] Monáe's transmedia project *Dirty Computer* is central to this chapter, as the first of her albums to express an explicitly queer Black perspective. This analysis is complemented by discussions of the TV series *I May Destroy You* and *Homecoming*, each of which deepens our understanding of intersectionality's networked and decentered paradigm. From this perspective, her work serves as a powerful example of how intersectionality offers not just a way of understanding the matrix of domination, but also an illustration of how the networked organization of digital media offers new opportunities for queer Black activism.

The fourth vector is that of posthumanism—a term I situate explicitly in relation to the ways in which Western definitions of the human have always been racialized.[24] Central in this chapter is Monáe's recurrent use of cyborg/android tropes throughout her work to destabilize the human/nonhuman divide. As an entry point, I discuss "Autofac," a TV episode in which Monáe plays an android trying to contain a (post)human rebellion. The chapter next turns to Monáe's ongoing performance of her alter ego, the android Cindi Mayweather. Her creative use of cyborgs, androids, and dirty computers constitutes a challenge to liberal humanism's social hierarchy, as they come to function as a provocative stand-in for racialized and gendered forms of dehumanization.[25] As a central term in this chapter, *plasticity*[26] helps clarify Monáe's use of androids and dirty computers—but also sheds light on the more literal plastic of cultural narratives surrounding children's toys, as in the animated film *UglyDolls* (2019).

The book's fifth and final vector is that of postcapitalism. As all the previous vectors erupt in different ways from racial capitalism's matrix of domination, this chapter brings together many of those threads. Considering how racial capitalism is the root cause of the various oppressions Monáe's work engages with, her liberating creative work is ultimately fueled by a postcapitalist imagination. This final chapter examines Monáe's protest songs "Hell You Talmbout" and "Turntables," and the utopian horizons she has projected within the context of her science fiction concept albums. The chapter concludes with a discussion of the key role that love plays in her creative work, and how it connects to a postcapitalist imagination. This analysis leads me back on the one hand to the Black utopian horizon that is central to Monáe's Afrofuturist project, and on the other to the thornier question of media production within the industrial realities of global capitalism. The chapter will therefore look on the one hand at how the representation of utopian futures expresses a postcapitalist political imaginary, and on the other at how Monáe's navigation of capitalist systems of media production also provide entrance points for transforming these systems from the inside out. Together, these five intersecting vectors articulate the powerful combination of creative, political, and theoretical energy that runs throughout Janelle Monáe's work, as they resonate across the larger network of social movements and popular culture.

This book thereby offers a study of a distinctive artist whose work brings together many of the key tensions that define our times. And while it is a work of cultural theory, I emphatically approach Monáe not as an object to analyze, but as a thinker whose creative work is engaged in an ongoing dialogue with activists, scholars, and other creative figures. It is therefore not an attempt to "apply" theory to a particular artist, but to embrace theory as "a breathing, changeable thing that can be infused in many political and artistic forms."[27] The book's thematic organization into five separate vectors provides points of entry for the ideas and political energies that have developed throughout Monáe's work as an artist, a thinker, and an activist.

As a white man writing about the work of a queer Black woman, I have been very conscious of the limitations this imposes throughout the writing process. While Monáe's creative output has certainly been enormously impactful for me at a personal level, I obviously cannot speak to the ways in which it resonates with those who have shared her lived experience of gendered and racialized oppression.[28] I have tried to avoid the traps of "mansplaining" or "whitesplaining" Monáe, seeking instead to amplify the voices of Black theorists, artists, and intellectuals like herself, while also relating them to voices from other domains.

By celebrating her work and placing it in dialogue with other theorists, artists, and media texts, this book aims to contribute to our understanding of the complex relationships between race, gender, and media power. Janelle Monáe's trailblazing work in the field of cultural production has been an inspiration to many—myself included. My hope for this book is that it will strengthen her impact and amplify her voice, and that it may stimulate others to engage with the queer Black feminist goals her work so powerfully expresses. In Monáe's own words: Power up!

Vector 1

████████████████████

Afrofuturism

Goooo-oo-ood morning, cy-boys and cyber-girls. I am happy to announce that we have a star-crossed lover in today's Heartbreak Sweepstakes: android number 57821, otherwise known as Cindi Mayweather, has fallen desperately in love with a human named Anthony Greendown. And you know the rules: she is now scheduled for immediate disassembly. Bounty hunters, you can find her in the Neon Valley Street district, on the fourth floor at the Leopard Plaza apartment complex. The Droid Control Marshals are full of fun rules today: no phasers, only chainsaws and electro-daggers! Remember: only card-carrying bounty hunters can join our chase today. And as usual, there will be no reward until her cyber-soul is

turned in to the Star Commission.
Happy hunting!

This announcement opens Monáe's first concept album, *Metropolis: The Chase Suite*, accompanied by symphonic strings, electronic beeps and gurgles, and a pounding militaristic drum roll. It instantly immerses the listener in a science fiction adventure story that opens in medias res, with the singer's android alter ego Cindi Mayweather on the run from the cops. This narrative hook, focused on an android who has fallen in love with a human being, combines the romantic convention of "star-crossed lovers" with dystopian science fiction. Monáe then uses these genre tropes to construct an allegorical storyworld about miscegenation, dehumanization, and other forms of racialized oppression.

As a Black performing artist whose work is full of images, narratives, and concepts drawn from science fiction, Monáe has been at the forefront of the twenty-first-century revival of *Afrofuturism*: a cultural movement that centers the identities and experiences of African Americans by kicking "preconceived ideas of blackness out of the solar system."[1] In 2018, the phenomenal success of Marvel movie *Black Panther* brought Afrofuturism definitively into the mainstream. But its way had been paved by the creative work of many Black writers, artists, performers, and musicians. Their Afrofuturism has explored what Black science fiction scholar André M. Carrington describes as *speculative Blackness*: the creative expression of Black diasporic identity that draws its power from "the generative quality of marginality in the popular imagination."[2]

Janelle Monáe's concept albums, stage performances, emotion pictures, and media appearances introduced a new generation to ideas that had first taken shape in the 1970s. She did this work not in isolation but as part of a larger vector of Black artists working across media: in the 2010s, Afrofuturism found literary acclaim in the novels of prolific authors like N. K. Jemisin, Colson Whitehead, Nnedi Okorafor, and Tade Thompson, and audiovisual representation in films and series like *Get Out* (2017), *Sorry to Bother You* (2018), *Us* (2019), *Watchmen* (2019), and *Lovecraft Country* (2020). In short, Monáe's world-building is part of a larger Afrofuturist vector that has reshaped debates about how we imagine a shared future in an anti-Black world. And as the global antiracist movement has gained new momentum, Afrofuturist art has clarified why so many white people still struggle to even acknowledge the basic fact that Black lives matter.

Monáe's remarkable contributions to this vector illustrate the deep connections between cultural production, racism, and antiracist activism. As her musical career has blossomed, she has expanded her speculative storyworld in ways that also strengthened her career as an actor and activist. The subsequent chapters in this book will explore how Monáe's work as a performer and activist has further expanded this vector—but her musical Afrofuturism forms the foundation upon which this is built. This chapter therefore first offers a brief account of Afrofuturism in the context of racial capitalism; then explains how its forms and structures strengthen a longer tradition of Black radicalism; and finally describes how Monáe's Afrofuturism rewires our understanding of the relationship between utopian and dystopian speculation.

Afrofuturism and Racial Capitalism

The term "Afrofuturism" was introduced in 1994 by white cultural theorist Mark Dery, who defined it as "speculative fiction that treats African-American themes and addresses African-American concerns in the context of 20th-century technoculture."[3] This definition provided a potent starting point for interrogating what it means to imagine Black futures in a cultural field governed by "the white historical mastery of time and space."[4] But subsequent theorists have expanded considerably on this initial definition. In his book *Afrofuturism Rising*, Isiah Lavender III describes Afrofuturism as a narrative practice that has given expression to the spatial and temporal dislocation of the African diaspora throughout literary history. His conclusion that Afrofuturism encapsulates "all black creativity in the western world"[5] may seem hyperbolic. But once we realize that "Black consciousness is the laborious and heretical process of freedom-making,"[6] we start to recognize why a movement devoted to imagining Black futures has taken up such a central place within twenty-first-century narrative culture.

Following Lavender's provocative lead also helps us perceive Afrofuturism as more than merely a science-fictional expression of the Black Atlantic experience.[7] Instead, we might approach it as a philosophical and theoretical lens that brings into focus the reciprocal relationship between speculative fiction and the long history of anti-Black racism. Rather than approaching it as a convenient term to delimit (and thereby ghettoize) science-fictional works centered on Blackness, Afrofuturism offers a conceptual framework that helps illuminate, challenge, and transform the ubiquitous power of whiteness. Afrofuturism therefore isn't just a subgenre of science fiction that happens to be preoccupied with race. Instead, it confronts us with the fact that *all* science fiction is fundamentally about race. Or, to put it more simply: speculating about the future of humanity is always-already speculating about the future of race.

Cedric J. Robinson's term "racial capitalism" constituted a similar intervention: a potent reminder that "the development, organization, and expansion of capitalist society pursued essentially racial directions."[8] His foundational work as a theorist and historian of Black radicalism[9] has documented in exhaustive detail how slavery and anti-Blackness were "historical and organic rather than adventitious or synthetic" in the development of global capitalism.[10] As a system of social relations, racial capitalism has been grounded in liberal humanism's systematic abjection of blackness.[11] Every failure to acknowledge race as a central component therefore implicitly strengthens white advantage,[12] as if capitalism wasn't irrevocably tied to systemic racism. Hence: *racial capitalism*.

By the same token, the neutral-sounding term "science fiction" reproduces an implicitly Eurocentric understanding of speculative fiction that reinforces from "the basic whiteness of science fiction."[13] I therefore propose the term "Eurofuturism" as an alternative, to emphasize how the culturally dominant forms of science fiction reinforce anti-Blackness.[14] If we understand Eurofuturism, then, as a cultural expression of white-centered industrial capitalism, Afrofuturism represents first a countermovement that critically interrogates racial capitalism—and, more specifically, illuminates how "Eurocentric humanism needs blackness as a prop in order to erect whiteness."[15] Second, it provides an alternate theory and philosophy of cultural politics that foregrounds racialized oppression in the construction of fictional storyworlds.

In this sense, Afrofuturism deviates sharply from Eurofuturism. Racial capitalism has always required social hierarchies that distinguish Black from white, subject from object, center from margin, human from inhuman.[16] In the same way, it has depended on narratives and mythologies that reproduce whiteness as a default identity.[17] In science fiction's many depictions of speculative futures, the genre has historically privileged racial capitalism's basic

FIG. 1 The back cover of Janelle Monáe's *Metropolis: The Chase Suite–Special Edition*.
© 2008, Bad Boy Records/Wondaland.

mechanism of primitive accumulation through imperialist expansion and racialized oppression.[18] And since Western fantastic fiction is dominated by its systematic demonization of Blackness as an inherently threatening "Dark Other,"[19] it takes conscious effort to reverse this dynamic, decolonize our vocabulary, and "re-story" our narrative culture.[20]

This re-storying process is central to Afrofuturism. It contributes to anti-racist movements by foregrounding the significance of race in futurist speculation. It bolsters the civic imagination by imagining alternatives to racial capitalism.[21] And it provides frameworks for speculation that are drawn from histories of the oppressed, rather than those of the oppressor. As Robinson once wrote, "What is required for the African Diaspora to assume its historical significance is a new and different philosophy and a new theory of history."[22] Afrofuturism helps us imagine a great variety of such philosophies and theories of history, while teaching us how they find expression in the stories we tell.

Therefore, beyond seeing it either as a cultural form that expresses African American identity,[23] as speculative fiction that emanates from the Black Atlantic historical experience,[24] or as a narrowly defined subgenre of science fiction,[25] I instead embrace "Afrofuturism" as a term that grounds speculative fiction in our real-world histories of anti-Black racism and white supremacy. In short, Afrofuturism provides a narrative framework for world-building in which the Eurocentric assumptions of liberal humanism are radically reconfigured. Janelle Monáe has explored a variety of these energies and ideas in her work across media, beginning with the storyworld she developed in the concept albums and emotion pictures that together make up her "*Metropolis* cycle."

Janelle Monáe's Afrofuturist Storyworld

Monáe's major-label debut *Metropolis: The Chase Suite* (hereafter *Metropolis*)[26] was released on Sean "P. Diddy" Combs's Bad Boy Records in 2010 as a seven-track EP. The first four songs are situated entirely within the fictional world of a dystopian future that is richly illustrated in the strikingly elaborate liner notes.[27] These notes identify this environment as the postapocalyptic "last great city" of Metropolis, a "decadent wonderland" set in the year 2719 and ruled over by "evil Wolfmasters." In this context, the album introduces us to the uniquely soulful Alpha Platinum 9000-model Cindi Mayweather—android number 57821—who is condemned to immediate disassembly. Her crime: falling in love with the "dashing human named Anthony Greendown."

The basic premise of situating a forbidden android–human romance in a dystopian future offers fertile ground for an Afrofuturist storyworld anchored by a clear allegorical structure. The most obvious one would be that of miscegenation: even without any explicit mention of Greendown's race, the notion of a free and "fully human" man falling in love with a nonhuman slave inevitably evokes antimiscegenation laws. At the same time, the fact that Cindi is the one who is forced to go on the run cannily illustrates how oppressions of race and gender are fundamentally interwoven.[28]

And finally, the grounding concept of illegal love between two adult sexual partners resonates as an allegory for queerness—particularly as written and performed by someone as strikingly queer as Janelle Monáe.[29]

Metropolis's Monáe album cover, liner notes, and spoken introduction vividly established the basic contours of this Afrofuturist storyworld. The following three tracks—"Violet Stars Happy Hunting!!!," "Many Moons," and "Cybertronic Purgatory"—make up the narrative payload of the EP's eponymous Chase Suite. The first two plunge us headlong into this futuristic cityscape that Cindi navigates as she outruns her pursuers, while proving Hanif Abdurraqib's thesis that an album's opening should be "a loud and all-consuming stretch of madness."[30] "Violet Stars Happy Hunting!!!" is bursting with sound effects and spoken exclamations ("Don't let her get out the window!") that emphasize the concept album's narrative register, while the lyrics offer a dramatic first-person reflection of Cindi's trajectory as a fugitive ("I'm a slave girl without a race / On the run cause they're here to erase and chase out my kind"). The track then segues seamlessly into "Many Moons," which largely takes the form of a call-and-response between Monáe's lead vocals and her multitracked background chorus. This vocal multiplicity reflects the lyric's thematic contents, as the song expands Cindi's personal experience of persecution to descriptions of the android population's collective oppression ("We're dancing free, but we're stuck here underground / And everybody trying to figure they way out").

While these two tracks introduce Cindi Mayweather's plight and the social context she inhabits, the "Many Moons" emotion picture expands the storyworld far beyond the contents of the album.[31] In this nearly seven-minute production, Monáe performs the song with her band on a stage overlooking an android auction in Metropolis. In this futuristic catwalk-cum-slave auction, we see a diverse group of colorful characters bid on a series of Alpha Platinum models, all performed by Monáe in a variety of costumes and hairstyles. Where the album's lyrics depict only Cindi's flight and the beginning of her transformation, director Alan Ferguson's video visualizes what the liner notes call her "rock-star proficiency package" as well as the effects of her "rebellious new form of pop music known as cybersoul." Thus, without adding to the narrative development mapped out—however minimally—on the album, the "Many Moons" emotion picture dramatically expands the storyworld.[32]

Then, as "Many Moons" comes to a close on the album, the propulsive momentum of the album's opening sequence abruptly shifts into the ethereal vocal distortions of "Cybertronic Purgatory." In a departure from the fast-paced alt-rock of the previous tracks, this third song opens in silence, an acoustic guitar and accordion slowly fading in to accompany Monáe's electronically distorted vocalizing. Expressionistically communicating Cindi's isolation, the track marks a radical shift in tempo, tone, and register that closes out this first narrative episode on the *Metropolis* album cycle. Monáe's operatic falsetto singing the brief lyric expresses the character's solitude, away from her lover ("Sorry I'm in a maze—No words do"). Thus, Cindi may have evaded her pursuers by the close of this brief track, but she is also painfully isolated from the romantic relationship that had led to her status as a fugitive.

But rather than ending there, the album shifts gears once again, taking us away from Cindi's Afrofuturist storyworld and its synth-heavy musical arrangements. Instead, the lush instrumentation of a full orchestra defines the sound of the next track, "Sincerely, Jane."[33] Mirroring this shift in arrangement, the song's lyric departs from Cindi Mayweather's futuristic environment. The track's title announces this change in perspective from twenty-eighth-century Cindi to twenty-first-century Janelle/Jane, while the lyric evokes the social realism of classic soul music as the "inappropriable result of oppression"[34]—not a science-fictional allegory in which sentient androids stand in for a racialized urban underclass, but vivid descriptions of Black urban life under the dystopian reality of racial capitalism. Many of the terms she uses to describe a contemporary reality of Black suffering ("All you gangers and bangers / Rolling dice and taking lives in a smoky dark") also recall the long list of associations in the rap section from "Many Moons" ("Heroin user, coke head / Final chapter, death bed")—now seemingly divorced from the album's Afrofuturist framework.

It is a reversal that Monáe will repeat with variations across her subsequent albums, as the creation of this elaborate and long-running storyworld is turned upside-down (or rather, right side up) to make its metaphorical structure more explicit. This reminds us insistently that fantastic worldbuilding only exists as a symbolic reflection of our material reality. J.R.R. Tolkien—the beloved fantasy author whose work is suspiciously popular among white supremacists—famously described the process of worldbuilding as "subcreation."[35] According to this concept, the author's imaginative work should yield a clear and stable boundary between the "Primary World" of reality and the "Secondary Worlds" of fantastic fiction.[36] The boundary between these two domains supposedly creates a membrane that allows for full immersion in the fantastic storyworld, which is organized according to its own internal logic.

But this membrane is an illusion—a lie, even. For Afrofuturists like Monáe, the fantasy helps us face reality in order to transform it. Her narratives, characters, and emotions stage an unavoidable confrontation with the racial organization of our social order. In other words, one of Afrofuturism's key functions is to short-circuit fantastic fiction's binary separating the myth of white innocence[37] from the racialized "positioning of the Dark Other as an antagonist."[38] The final about-face that concludes "Sincerely, Jane" and returns us once more to Cindi's world—a spoken outro in which android #57821 is called upon to return home—explicitly underlines the reciprocal relationship that binds these two worlds together.

This juxtaposition of seemingly contradictory time frames is no accident: it has been an essential strategy for Afrofuturist world-building. The way Monáe places her two worlds in dialogue with each other is thoroughly dialectical—which is to say, the relationship between her "real" and "fictional" selves establishes a tension that can never be fully resolved. Instead, it reveals a constant splitting of identity that contradicts the false universal subject of liberal humanism. This dialectical movement is guided by Afrofuturism's characteristic treatment of the fundamentally political organization of time.

Afrofuturist Chronopolitics

Consider for a moment the fantasy represented by *Back to the Future* (1985), the beloved classic in which middle-class white teenager Marty McFly time-travels from the 1980s to the 1950s to discover there a more innocent time of fun, excitement, and free-spirited adventure. Now try to imagine how different Marty's trip to Jim Crow–era Hill Valley would have been if he had been Black, and you instantly grasp how racial identity has an impact on time as a force of politics[39]—or, as visionary artist and theorist Kodwo Eshun has called it, *chronopolitics*.[40] This notion of temporality as irreducibly political has been fundamental to Afrofuturist mythologies, from Sun Ra's "MythScience" to Monáe's *Metropolis* cycle. Afrofuturist chronopolitics represents a force that "recognizes the ways African diasporans have long understood the sense of fracturing, disorientation, and alienation associated with modernity and holds an epistemology of the future that challenges a linear Western model of progress."[41]

Eurocentric historiography has been stubbornly linear, always forging ahead in search of new territories to conquer, new peoples to enslave, new resources to extract and exploit, and new technologies to appropriate, commodify, and weaponize. This colonialist mentality has operated by mapping capitalist notions of *time* onto *space*: the endless "New Worlds" required by capitalist expansion paradoxically represented a blank-slate future for white people, while indigenous peoples were assumed to represent a primitive, disposable, and inhuman past.[42] Western speculative fiction has projected this imperialist expansion further outward, as liberal humanism's core belief in progress through technological innovation fed a triumphalist narrative of white superiority.[43] Thus, even though this linear trajectory has also included momentary setbacks and disruptions, Eurofuturist science fiction has offered us an endless variety of narratives that present the future as yet another territory to be conquered.[44]

Afrofuturist chronopolitics expresses a strikingly different approach to concepts of time, memory, and power. White Europeans' genocidal abduction of African peoples constituted a real-life alien invasion, making enslaved Black people the first group to undergo a quite literal form of abduction by a technologically advanced invader.[45] At the same time, colonialism violently imposed capitalism's monolithic measurement of time across the globe, eradicating every alternative that deviates from its standard.[46] Seeing linear spacetime as a powerful form of control helps us recognize and understand how disruptions of racial capitalism's dictatorial continuum have been central to the Afrofuturist imagination.[47] Resisting and subverting this linear conception of temporal progression is therefore more than a cultural act of transformation: it is a radical political act that undermines the foundations of Western imperialism, white supremacy, and even racial capitalism itself.

Afrofuturism's transformative imagination has countered the existing realities that reinforce white power structures by focusing on Black utopias that disrupt linear spacetime.[48] This sense of simultaneously occupying multiple positions in a radically uneven distribution of spacetime can be seen as the science-fictional articulation of what W.E.B. Du Bois famously described as *double consciousness*: the experience felt by descendants of the African diaspora that Black subjectivity has been divided at its core, resulting in a fractured sense of identity.[49] For in the words of Achille Mbembe, "to be black means to be placed by the force of things on the side of those that go unseen, but that one nevertheless always permits oneself to represent."[50] This double consciousness, again, is entirely political. It is actively produced by a system of social relations in which whiteness has been established "as a *right to* geography, to *take* place, to *traverse* the globe and to *extract* from cultural, corporeal, and material registers."[51] With whiteness defined by ownership and appropriation, being Black means being deprived of past, present, and future—or, as Frantz Fanon phrased it: "Without a black past, without a black future, it was impossible for me to live my blackness."[52]

Afrofuturism translates this impossibility into a cultural form, a philosophy of history, and a creative method. By foregrounding the relationship between race, power, and time, Afrofuturist chronopolitics foregrounds how whiteness operates as an "absent center against which others appear only as deviants, or points of deviation."[53] Black American poet and performance artist Gil Scott-Heron articulated this "Othered" status in his track "Evolution (and Flashback)," a polemical reflection on the dehumanizing categorizations white people inflicted upon him and his ancestors across history:

> In 1600 I was a darkie
> And until 1865 a slave
> In 1900 I was a nigger
> Or at least that was my name
> In 1960 I was a negro
> And then Malcolm came along
> Yes, but some nigger shot Malcolm down
> Though the bitter truth lives on
> Well now I am a black man
> And though I still go second-class
> Whereas once I wanted the white man's love
> Now he can kiss my ass

This verse starkly demonstrates how "racial differentiation constituted the grounds on which claims to rationality, rights, self-rule, and national standing were imagined as simultaneously universal and delimited."[54] Imagining futures that center Black lives therefore invariably necessitates a rewriting of history. Afrofuturist re-storying reclaims a past that has been appropriated by whiteness—in science fiction as much as in Western historiography.

Octavia E. Butler's breakthrough 1979 novel *Kindred* provides an illuminating example of Afrofuturism's temporal multidirectionality.[55] The book's protagonist Dana, a young Black woman living in 1976 Los Angeles, finds herself becoming "unstuck in time" as she is involuntarily catapulted back and forth between her relatively comfortable twentieth-century environment and a pre–Civil War plantation. Science-fictional only in its (unexplained) use of time travel as a narrative device, the novel's unsettling exploration of race, gender, and power perfectly dramatizes the chronopolitical nature of Du Boisian double consciousness. This finds expression through Dana's realization that the abusive white boy she meets in the past turns out to be her own ancestor. In order to make possible her entire family's existence, she is therefore condemned to protect the life of her own abuser, and the rapist of her great-great-great-grandmother. The novel hereby emphasizes the complicated ways in which the horrors of the past not only live on in the present, but that they also mark us as complicit in their horrific legacy.[56]

Throughout her career, Janelle Monáe has adopted a similarly chronopolitical approach to her Afrofuturist world-building. Smoothly integrating time travel into her speculative storyworld, her transformation of this well-worn trope emphasizes how movement through time represents rather different possibilities for anyone who isn't white. As Noel Ignatiev famously wrote, white supremacy underlies the rule of the bourgeoisie, marking Black people as perpetual objects of pursuit.[57] Just as Colson Whitehead's Afrofuturist novel *The Underground Railroad* dislocates enslaved Black fugitives from linear spacetime,[58] Monáe's chronopolitical Afrofuturism has systematically challenged clear distinctions between past, present, and future. Her starring role in the Afrofuturist horror film *Antebellum* (2020) vividly illustrates this approach.

Antebellum: "The Past Is Never Dead"

When the teaser trailer for *Antebellum* dropped in November 2019, the internet was instantly abuzz. The 59-second video[59] seemed to juxtapose two historical periods: one in which we see Janelle Monáe enslaved on a southern plantation, and one in which we see her enjoying an upper middle-class life in the present. The provocative teaser inspired tremendous speculation: would the film be a variation on *Kindred*, featuring a contemporary Black woman involuntarily time-traveling to America's horrific past of chattel slavery? Would she play two separate characters, juxtaposing two separate time periods? Or would there be some other narrative trick through which America's enduring legacy of slavery would be connected to the contemporary social organization of racial capitalism?

When the film was finally released in September 2020 after several pandemic-induced delays, the plot turned out to hinge not on time travel but on a different form of temporal dislocation. The first of the film's three distinct segments appears to take place on a plantation in the pre–Civil War South, where Monáe plays an enslaved woman called Eden. While one may notice a number of odd anachronisms, like the sight of torch-bearing Confederate soldiers chanting the Nazi phrase "blood and soil," the first part has the familiar trappings of a slavery-era rape-revenge film. This section ends abruptly when the jarringly anachronistic sound of a ringing cell phone signals the transition to the film's second segment, where Monáe plays a celebrated scholar–activist named Veronica Henley, who's about to leave her doting family to promote her new book.

As the film follows Henley on her trip to Louisiana, the film focuses our attention on the everyday microaggressions that reinforce white supremacy: the unmistakable look of annoyance when she asks the hotel desk clerk to make dinner reservations, a waiter seating her party at the worst able in the restaurant, and other common expressions of what Achille Mbembe describes as "nanoracism."[60] Then, at the very end of this sequence, we see Henley being kidnapped and forced to participate in a large-scale reenactment of slavery-era plantation life. This plot twist brings us to the third and last part, as we return to the same plantation where we have already seen her undergo horrific physical and sexual abuse. As we realize that this plantation is a secret theme park for cosplaying racists, this last sequence shows Eden/Elizabeth organizing a daring escape, which ultimately leads to the covert organization's exposure and the destruction of the fascist LARPers' compound.

Thus, even though *Antebellum* sidesteps explicitly science-fictional tropes like time travel or supernatural doppelgängers,[61] the script deftly mobilizes Afrofuturism's central focus on chronopolitics. William Faulkner's famous lines "The past is never dead. It's not even past" appear first as an on-screen epigram and later in the characters' dialogue, unsubtly underlining the deep historical roots of anti-Black racism and the double consciousness this long history has produced. The film's chronopolitical organization thereby offers another way of expressing what Christina Sharpe has called the enduring *wake* left behind by New World slavery. Her words on this topic are worth quoting at length:

> Living in the wake means living the history and present of terror, from slavery to the present, as the ground of our everyday Black existence; living the historically and geographically dis/continuous but always present and endlessly reinvigorated brutality in, and on, our bodies while even as that terror is visited on our bodies the realities of that terror are erased. Put another way, living in the wake means living in and with terror in that in much of what passes for public discourse *about* terror we, Black people, become the *carriers* of terror, terror's embodiment, and not the primary objects of terror's multiple enactments, the ground of terror's possibility globally.[62]

Sharpe uses the double meaning of the word "wake" here to indicate the indelible rift created by the violence of racial capitalism, even as it is simultaneously denied by a system of white social power that is unwilling to even acknowledge the terror it continuously inflicts.

Afrofuturist chronopolitics translates the wake left by histories of institutional racism into new possibilities for Black futures. The Black Atlantic's undying social and cultural wake is *Antebellum*'s clear focus—and even if the film places too much emphasis on the depiction of Black suffering,[63] it also illustrates how Afrofuturism is as much about the past as it is about the future. In the film's most memorable sequence, Monáe's character escapes the compound on horseback, wearing a Union army jacket and wielding a battle-axe, her face distorted into a defiant snarl as she looks back on her past while forging a path toward her own "uplifting revolution."[64] The moment shows numerous lines of history intersecting and combusting, as her ferocious charge opens up new pathways toward a horizon of liberation and possibility.

It is a great moment and a fine performance in a film that also demonstrates the minefield that stories like these must navigate. Where similarly themed productions like *Get Out* and the TV series *Watchmen* have largely succeeded in translating Afrofuturist chronopolitics into popular narratives,[65] *Antebellum* was sharply criticized for being simultaneously exploitative

FIG. 2 *Antebellum*, directed by Gerard Bush and Christopher Renz. © 2020 Lionsgate.

of and didactic about Black suffering.[66] As so often, these moments show how Hollywood's slave narratives resort to the "enactment of black suffering for a shocked and titillated audience" that so often provides the template for cinematic depictions of chattel slavery.[67] At the same time, these criticisms sharpen our awareness of how limited American popular culture has been in meaningfully addressing anti-Blackness. This lack of a popular archive of antiracist narratives continues to pose challenges for Afrofuturist storytellers in film and television.

Little wonder then that the more fluid forms of popular music have been much more productive for Afrofuturist speculation and experimentation. In this sense, Monáe's work is primarily situated within a longer history of *sonic Afrofuturism*.

Sonic Afrofuturism

In the wake of the post-war civil rights movement, sonic Afrofuturism has pioneered forms of expression that joined the creation of speculative storyworlds with the Black radical tradition.[68] In particular, George Clinton's P-Funk collective, consisting of the overlapping musical groups Parliament and Funkadelic, transformed jazz visionary Sun Ra's space-oriented "Astro Black Mythology" into an infectiously funk-driven science fiction storyworld.[69] Across a legendary series of albums, stage performances, and visual supplements in the form of comics, album covers, and animated cartoons, Clinton's "Funketeers" developed an expansive Afrofuturist mythology[70] that fused Black radicalism with fantastic storytelling.[71] Collectively, the group's "funkology" loosely followed the adventures of the character Starchild and his motley crew of colorful freaks on board the Mothership.[72] Both on stage and off, the collective used the mystical force of Funkentel-echy and the unifying power of "da groove" to defeat arch-villain Sir Nose D'Voidoffunk, leading all of humanity toward a Black utopian horizon.[73]

Similar Afrofuturist motifs proliferated across Black popular music genres from the late 1960s onward. Glowing pyramids, glittering space suits, and cosmological iconography figured prominently in the album covers and stage shows of groups like Earth, Wind and Fire,[74] Miles Davis's jazz-rock fusion on *Bitches Brew*,[75] the Jimi Hendrix Experience's soaring double album *Electric Ladyland*,[76] Stevie Wonder's unrivaled cycle of adventurous 1970s soul albums,[77] and the financially unsuccessful but enduringly influ-ential Hollywood musical *The Wiz* (1978).[78]

This explosive outburst of Black musical innovation was followed by a reactionary countermovement in the 1980s, in which many of these pioneers were pushed back to the margins and the American music industry was largely resegregated.[79] But even in this neoconservative period of Reagan-era whitelash, many Black musicians continued to draw on Afrofuturist energies, especially in the music videos that dominated the MTV era: Billy Ocean's 1985 hit "Lover Boy" featured a *Star Wars*–inspired assortment of aliens[80]; Tupac and Dr. Dre populated the postapocalyptic Thunderdome from the *Mad Max* franchise with Black partygoers in "California Love (Remix)"[81]; Janet Jackson led a futuristic army of hard-stepping revolution-aries in "Rhythm Nation"[82]; and of course her brother Michael employed fantastic tropes and elaborate Afrofuturist imagery throughout his career[83]—most notably in his Egyptian-themed "Remember the Time"[84] and his retro-futuristic collaboration with his sister, "Scream."[85] But each of these instances entailed little more than a single moment of performa-tive play-acting: incidental appropriations that placed Black performers within a mass cultural genre that remained stubbornly white.[86]

The twenty-first-century Afrofuturist revival is in the process of chang-ing this.[87] Janelle Monáe built up her musical career by embracing the tra-dition established by P-Funk's ambitious world-building. Like P-Funk's expansive mythology, Monáe's android character of Cindi Mayweather has continuously developed alongside her own public persona throughout her career. This has given her the ability to extend, enrich, and revise her story-world and its inhabitants in dialogue with the outside world—while also crossing over to other media.[88]

In doing so, she has taken full advantage of the increasingly networked organization of convergence culture in the digital age.[89] But it is also important to differentiate her unusually elaborate sonic Afrofuturism from the immersive narrative universes that have proliferated over recent years to fully dominate our media landscape.[90] The creators of sonic Afrofuturism construct speculative storyworlds—just as the authors and producers of countless novels, videogames, and movie franchises do. But the type of performance in music videos and pop music tracks is fundamentally different from that of traditional narrative film and television. Even extended productions like Michael Jackson's 13-minute "Thriller"[91] music video have only limited means of establishing things like character, plot, and setting, and therefore must rely more strongly on stereotypes, clichés, and intertextuality as a form of narrative shorthand. Even more importantly, music videos developed industrially and institutionally as media objects with the primary function of promoting a particular song and its performer.[92] Their production costs are typically funded by the record company's promotional budget, and they therefore exist by definition as secondary to the product being sold: the musical track and its performing artist as celebrity-commodity.[93] This material reality has strongly determined the aesthetics of the music video as a textual form in which the *absolute primacy of the performer-as-star* overshadows each attempt to perform a fictional character.[94]

This primacy takes formal shape in the music video performer's characteristic fourth-wall-breaking gaze into the camera.[95] The music video star acknowledges the audience by looking us right in the eye, returning the camera's gaze, irrespective of their performance or character within that particular video. Unlike the movie star, who is trained to avoid acknowledging the camera's voyeuristic gaze at all costs, the music video star insistently stares back at us.[96] Their celebrity is therefore in many ways the "primary product," bestowing value on a wide range of secondary commodities.[97] And their mesmerizing gaze binds us to them in mutual awareness of their ambiguous commodity status, defiantly yelling into the camera and flaunting their bodies and sexuality with a "conviction that renders them invincible."[98]

While this may diminish our sense of immersion in a fictional storyworld, it also opens up a more radical space for fluidity and multiplicity that we rarely encounter in other narrative media forms. Just as David Bowie's on-stage performance of alien visitor Ziggy Stardust allowed him to disrupt normative gender roles, other pop artists—from Janet Jackson and Mariah Carey to Miley Cyrus and Beyoncé—have explored the music video's radical potential as a form that's "capable of reinvigorating our critical and political imagination."[99] The explicit artificiality of pop music celebrity makes it easier to mock, subvert, and negotiate social norms relating to gender, race, and sexual identity. Or, as Paul Gilroy observed about pop music's productive slipperiness: "Music and its rituals can be used to create a model whereby identity can be understood neither as a fixed essence nor as a vague and utterly contingent construction to be reinvented by the will and whim of aesthetes, symbolists, and language gamers."[100] In other words, pop music performance offers an unusually rich terrain for the "crossing of generic boundaries of form or the crossing of gender or racial boundaries" through self-conscious modes of performative eccentricity.[101]

A second key difference that sets apart Monáe's android alter ego from something like Chadwick Boseman's performance of Black Panther is the question of *intellectual property*. For as Boseman's untimely death so tragically underlined, he will ultimately be just one of several human performers to inhabit a character that is part of a bundle of IP owned and operated by a global media corporation. The film's utopian Afrofuturism may endure within a single film, but it will inevitably be dissolved as the Marvel media behemoth lumbers on indifferently.[102] In this sense, it is one thing for the Disney-owned Marvel Studios to hire Ryan Coogler to helm the production of this rare majority-Black blockbuster. But it is quite another for an artist of color to own the rights to their own storyworld, to determine its development independent from any larger media franchise, and to develop this in collaboration with a collective of similar-minded and wholly autonomous Black artists.

As a case in point, Janelle Monáe is not just the person who happens to perform the role of Cindi Mayweather. She is also in charge of her creation, development, and narrative progression, which she has developed in collaboration with her Atlanta-based Wondaland Arts Society.[103] At a basic level, this affects our understanding of the character's nature in relation not just to her own storyworld but also to Monáe's role as author/creator. This question of ownership is fundamental to Afrofuturism as a creative, cultural, and political movement in the context of racial capitalism. The artistic autonomy of Monáe's storyworld is therefore even more essential in a context where the development of cultural icons is increasingly determined by the financial imperatives of global media conglomerates. This yields an artist-owned serialized storyworld that has been free to develop in dialogue with Monáe's own interests as an artist, thinker, and activist, as the rest of this book will further illustrate. But it also incorporates an Afrofuturist approach that builds upon a longer tradition of Black utopianism.

Black Utopias

The specter of utopia has haunted science fiction since its very inception. White modernity fostered the illusion of linear progress and boundless expansion, projecting flying-car futures where white people lived like middle-class gods. The notion that European civilizations were headed toward a point of godlike mastery was a predictable extension of this way of thinking. While utopian speculation obviously predates science fiction, the specifically modernist idea of engineering the perfect society through technological innovation and territorial expansion was central to the development of racial capitalism, and its energy has strongly marked the science fiction genre to this day.

Little wonder then that the modernist architecture featured in Fritz Lang's *Metropolis* (1927) still casts its long shadow over the genre's depiction of futuristic cityscapes.[104] As twentieth-century attempts to engineer ideal societies repeatedly failed, this sensibility ultimately gave way to visions of abortive utopias: speculative worlds in which the breakdown of modernity paved the way to a new romantic primitivism. But while the assumption of disastrous futures has incontrovertibly become the norm for post-1960s science fiction, it is important to remember that dystopia is not the reverse—or even the negation—of utopia, but rather its dialectical counterpart: dystopian futures are explicitly *failed utopias*, as they document tendencies in actually existing Western societies playing out in emphatically undesirable ways.

The two most celebrated anglophone dystopias—Aldous Huxley's *Brave New World* (1932) and George Orwell's *1984* (1949)—depict utopian societies gone disastrously wrong. In both books, the modernist pathology toward top-down hierarchies and omnipresent mass media paves the way toward totalitarianism and the negation of liberal humanist values. Eurofuturism's many more recent dystopias, from *Soylent Green* (1973) to *The Circle* (2013), have indeed repeated countless variations on a basic pattern: a white, male protagonist becomes aware of the oppressive nature of his society, which leads him to rebel against it. As a result, he is: (1) tragically crushed by the system he has opposed; (2) martyred so his sacrifice might inspire a rebellion; or (3) successful in restoring utopia. But whatever the outcome, these dystopian futures project the "universal" human subject through the lens of white masculinity, which remains somehow blameless for the utopia's original failure.

This supposed oversight is all the more glaring due to the notorious absence of people of color in the Eurofuturist canon. For while intensified debates on diversity have surely made a difference in recent years, one is still too easily reminded of Richard Pryor's acidic comment on the genre's pernicious whiteness from 1976: "I don't like movies when they ain't have no [Black people][105] in it. I went to see *Logan's Run*, right? They had a movie of the future called *Logan's Run*? There ain't no [Black people] in it! I said: well, white folks ain't planning for us to be here!"[106] In a context where cultural production has churned out futures in which Black people either don't exist at all or only as barely present background figures,[107] we can see why Afrofuturist utopias require "a complete break with time as we know it."[108] Rather than articulating modernism's linear drive toward total mastery, Black utopias have constituted a mixture of "pragmatic experimentation and critical reexamination"[109] that challenges the idea that the future is merely "the contiguous culmination of preceding actions."[110]

By the same token, the Black utopian tradition is steeped in a double movement that combines the critical deconstruction of white supremacy with the "utopian transformation of racial subordination."[111] This facilitates a *redemptive critique* that opens up pathways toward futures that offer a promise of real freedom. And since this redemptive critique emerges in dialogue with memories of the racist and colonialist past, it is shaped by dreams of escape rather than fantasies of expansion. This is, again, why the Afrofuturist imaginary is so much more than the expression of Black speculative futures. If the overarching goal is not the expansion of power but the eradication of oppression, then we can see how Afrofuturism is uniquely able to project a utopian horizon that is truly universal.

This is all the more necessary at a time when racial capitalism's many interlocking crises have made the very idea of a hopeful future increasingly difficult to imagine.[112] As catastrophic climate change, resurgent fascism, escalating political crises, and the inevitable fracturing of global neoliberal hegemony strike us in the back of the head like a boomerang, the well of Eurofuturist optimism has truly run dry.[113] Ironically, our current age of digital capitalism is ruled not by dreams of a better future but by "an ideology of the future *now*, which in turn paralyzes all thought about the future."[114] Many commentators have indeed observed that the crisis of the Anthropocene is at its core a failure of imagination.[115] And as we slowly realize that the ways of thinking that got us into this mess aren't very useful for imagining a way out, Eurofuturism is no longer able to generate credible visions of the future—just as neoliberal capitalism's faltering hegemony almost inevitably cedes ground to ethnonationalist movements.[116]

Afrofuturism, on the other hand, has consistently articulated *alternate* histories by imagining "impossible trajectories of Black freedom."[117] These trajectories reject dominant Western historiographies that are ultimately grounded in the reproduction of white supremacy. But this freedom is more than freedom from chattel slavery, from Jim Crow segregation, or from colonial systems of domination: it is also the freedom to define one's own identity and reject the foundational Othering that has historically reproduced the multiple oppressions that are irreducibly inherent in the system of racial capitalism. This double movement is condensed most acutely in Monáe's transmedia project *Dirty Computer*—a project that I discuss in more detail in Vector 3, but which I will first introduce here to describe how its narrative incorporates Afrofuturism's chronopolitical organization.

Dirty Computer

Janelle Monáe's fourth album was the first to step outside her established Afrofuturist framework of her *Metropolis* cycle. Listening to *Dirty Computer*, there appears to be little sign of the elaborate world-building Monáe undertook on her previous concept albums: no scene-setting orchestral overtures, no radio DJs interjecting bits of narrative commentary, no futuristic street names or devices—not even any mention of Cindi Mayweather or the Android Uprising.[118]

But the Afrofuturism that seemed absent from the album is generously provided by the forty-eight-minute emotion picture that was released alongside it on April 27, 2018.[119] The film opens with a montage of human bodies—Black and white, man and woman, naked and clothed—emerging and then disappearing within a smoke-filled vacuum. Over these images, Monáe narrates an introduction to this new dystopian environment: "They started calling us computers. People began vanishing, and the cleaning began. You were dirty if you looked different. You were dirty if you refused to live the way they dictated. You were dirty if you showed any form of

opposition at all. And if you were dirty, it was only a matter of time . . ."
This leads into *Dirty Computer*'s title caption, after which we see Monáe's
body strapped to a floating gurney being pushed down a hallway by a
quartet of masked orderlies who represent the totalitarian New Dawn
organization. After entering a larger space and tilting the gurney into a
forward-facing position, one of the masked figures places a helmet-shaped
electronic device over her head. Meanwhile, two white men in a booth
behind a window are seen preparing a device called the "Memmotron." A
female voice instructs her via loudspeakers to repeat a number of lines
acknowledging that her name is Jane 57821, that she is a "dirty computer,"
and that she is ready to be cleaned. When Monáe's character—whose name
combines the singer's own identity with the serial number associated with
her android alter ego—cannot speak those last words willingly, the voice
instructs the men to commence the "cleaning process" by initiating something called the NeverMind.

Once the bored-looking bureaucrats behind the glass launch the software,
the film's narrative structure takes shape: the technicians use the machine
to view Jane's memories, which we then access in audiovisual form before
they are casually deleted. Eight such sequences make up the body of the film,
each presented as a specific memory just before it is wiped out. This frame
narrative allows for a tremendous diversity of style across these multiple
musical sequences, which together sketch out a slender but effective narrative of polyamorous pansexuality, political resistance, and transgressive
experimentation.[120]

The emotion picture's narrative supports this with an ending that offers
the clearest illustration of Afrofuturist chronopolitics. As Jane 57821's memory is gradually wiped by the NeverMind technicians, she pleads with the
woman who's supervising her transition to halt the process. This character,
played by Tessa Thompson, introduces herself as "Mary Apple 53," but we
recognize her as Zen—one of Jane 57821's two lovers who had previously
been captured as a Dirty Computer and undergone a similar form of "cleaning." While Zen's visibly distraught response indicates that her recondi-
tioning is at least somewhat incomplete, she nevertheless appears to proceed
with the invasive procedure. After Jane then undergoes the traumatic final
phase of her cleaning, we next see her introducing herself as "Mary Apple
54" to the latest subject to arrive at the facility—a Black man we recognize
from the memory sequences as Jane's male lover Ché. This ending suggests
the completion of a bleak cycle of mental conditioning, as Jane 57821 becomes

the next "torch" to light the way for the next Dirty Computer's invasive reprogramming.

But this bleakly dystopian finale is followed by a different ending. After the screen cuts to black and the first end credits are displayed, patient viewers are rewarded with an additional sequence in which Jane and Zen reveal that they have been play-acting. They first deploy the NeverMind gas to incapacitate their captors, then assist a stumbling and half-conscious Ché outward toward freedom.[121] This alternative ending embraces with abandon what utopian theorist Ernst Bloch described as the "principle of hope"[122]: watching the polyamorous threesome finally flee New Dawn's conversion therapy facility and pass through the doorway into the outside world's blinding light becomes a gesture of true potentiality, articulating a temporality that is "not in the present but, more nearly, in the horizon, which we can understand as futurity."[123]

The ethereal white light into which the three of them disappear one by one represents utopian futurity as a field of potentiality.[124] At the same time, the invitation to participate that ends the album is reproduced in another register by Monáe's brief pause before she follows the two others out the door: she stops just before she exits the building while the camera moves in to her face. Framed in a tight close-up shot, she turns around slowly to stare back into the camera—an almost imperceptible smile playing on her lips as she finally steps out of focus and disappears into the blinding light of utopian possibility.

These two consecutive endings bring up questions that are central to Black utopias: does the second sequence negate the first ending? Is one of

FIG. 3 *Janelle Monáe: Dirty Computer*, directed by Andrew Donoho and Chuck Lightning. © 2018 Wondaland Pictures.

them real, and the other a dream (or a nightmare)? Is the characters' escape actual or only imagined? The emotion picture's deliberate ambiguous ending leaves the answers up to us. Instead, it allows utopian and dystopian visions to exist side by side. This expresses the painful tension at the core of Black utopian speculation. The utopian horizon it projects is one of freedom from oppression, but this tentative freedom is both terrifying and beautiful: "Its terror can lead to the valorization of arbitrary authority, but its beauty can lead to greater equality."[125]

Thus, while *Dirty Computer* doesn't directly reproduce the storyworld from Monáe's *Metropolis* cycle, its world-building builds upon the same central tension. Where the android narrative served as a powerful metaphor for racial capitalism's oppressive social hierarchy, the *Dirty Computer* project focuses our attention even more pointedly on the chronopolitical relationship between power and time. The disturbing violence inherent in the destruction of Jane 57821's memories constitutes an assault on her perception of temporality, identity, and community. Her resistance to this violence, and her surprising ability to transcend New Dawn's nightmarish forms of thought control, represent the optimism derived from the stubborn collective belief in a utopian future of freedom from oppression.[126]

Rather than marking a departure from her previous work, *Dirty Computer* therefore doubles down on Afrofuturism's chronopolitical dynamic. By incorporating the use of technology as a way to dominate Black consciousness, Monáe expands on her previous use of time travel and android bodies as allegories for white supremacy. The eradication of Jane 57821's memories of collective resistance thereby mirrors the deletion of Black narratives from Western histories.[127] This deep contradiction of simultaneous existence and nonexistence articulates the dialectical organization of Afrofuturist world-building: the expression of Black utopian futurity is framed from within the long history of racial capitalism's dystopian oppression.

2

Vector 2

■■■■■■■■■■■■■■■■■■■■■■■

Black Feminism

"One pattern of suppression is that of omission."[1] With this short phrase, Black feminist scholar Patricia Hill Collins perfectly summarized how deeply the oppressive structures of racism and sexism are grounded in media visibility. Many activists and critics often use the more colloquial phrase "you can't be what you can't see"[2] to point out the importance of media representation. Hollywood in particular has an atrocious historical record in the ways it has omitted people of color from its representation of the world we live in.[3] These deliberate crimes of omission have systematically devalued and underrepresented stories about Black people in general, and Black women in particular.[4]

Hidden Figures was a rare exception to this general practice. The Hollywood adaptation of Black historian Margot Lee Shetterly's book[5] dramatizes the stories of three Black women who worked as NASA mathematicians and engineers in the early years of America's space program. It shows them overcoming the many barriers of the Jim Crow era to develop careers as "human computers." And as its title announces, the film presents their inspirational narrative of Black feminist accomplishment as an explicit corrective to a dramatically incomplete historical record.

Co-starring alongside Taraji P. Henson and Octavia Spencer, Janelle Monáe appeared in the hit film in her breakout role as Mary Jackson—the first Black woman to work as a NASA engineer.[6] Her second on-screen performance and her first in a major studio production,[7] *Hidden Figures* gave Monáe tremendous visibility, while the film's Space Age setting seemed to extend naturally from Monáe's established image as an Afrofuturist artist and musician. But the movie's thematic focus on the often-invisible labor of Black women also underlined an aspect of Monáe's work that had been less prominent until then. Through its emphatic centering of Black women's struggles, the film's success foregrounded the powerful social and political movement of Black feminism as a second major vector in Janelle Monáe's career.

Black Women vs. White Saviors

Hidden Figures was a sizable holiday-season hit, ratcheting up a handful of Oscar nominations and boasting the strongest box office results among that year's crop of Best Picture nominees.[8] Its impact, prestige, and popular perception were further bolstered by the many free screenings that were organized to promote interest in STEM (science, technology, engineering, and math) fields, particularly among young Black women.[9] This indicates how strongly *Hidden Figures* was positioned as more than mere entertainment. While the script follows a comfortable formula in its dramatization of historical events, the movie served an explicitly didactic social and cultural function in educating audiences about the erasure of Black women's labor from historical records. In this sense, the film clearly contributes to the political project of Black feminism.

At the same time, there is something a little ridiculous about describing a stubbornly middlebrow entertainment in these terms. Like so many other socially engaged Hollywood productions before it, *Hidden Figures* goes out of its way to make white audiences comfortable. And like many others, it does so by adding a white savior figure to its central narrative: in the film's wholly fabricated emotional climax, the stern but benevolent patriarchal manager played by Kevin Costner takes a crowbar to the "Colored Ladies Room" sign before instructing his adoring staff to desegregate the bathrooms. This once again gives a white man credit for gains achieved through Black women's antiracist struggles—and it speaks volumes about how the movie's white director, screenwriter, and producer imagine their primary audience.

A movie like *Hidden Figures* thereby focuses our attention on the fraught relationship between mainstream culture and radical social movements.[10] Can a movie in which historical figures and events are fictionalized almost beyond recognition really strengthen Black feminism's radical social and political agenda? Do the culture industry's commercial entertainment commodities serve white liberal audiences far more potently than they do Black feminists' political agenda of meaningful social change? Are mainstream movie audiences likely to be substantially transformed by sentimental crowd-pleasers that serve up reassuring clichés about race and gender?

From *Guess Who's Coming to Dinner* (1967) to *Green Book* (2018), liberal Hollywood movies have depicted racism not as an urgent social issue that requires political action, but as an individual affliction that affects misguided white people.[11] Black characters in these movies suffer the indignities of racialized oppression in order to enlighten and transform white men, who may then redeem themselves by coming to the rescue of helpless Black victims. An entire subgenre of prestigious Oscar-winners like *Driving Miss Daisy* (1989), *The Blind Side* (2009), and *The Help* (2011) shows white middle-class women valiantly learning to overcome their own prejudice by befriending and supporting a Black person whose existence had barely registered as human with them. These white savior narratives are clearly not designed to document and expose the ways in which systemic racism remains embedded in our society.[12] Instead, they serve to make liberal white audiences feel better about themselves—usually by depicting narratives focused on past events, thus strengthening the reassuring fantasy of liberal humanist progress that facilitates postracial fantasies of already having moved "beyond racism."[13]

In other words, while *Hidden Figures* may justifiably pride itself for celebrating the largely undervalued achievements of Black women, it does so in ways that remain maximally comfortable and reassuring to white viewers. And adding insult to injury, it does so by reproducing the reassuring liberal fantasy that civil rights advances were primarily made by white male savior figures, whose lives are transformed by their enlightening interaction with dignified and demure Black women.

But as disappointing as the film is in its adherence to white liberalism's dominant structures of sympathy,[14] the film is also more than the sum of its ideological parts. A major Hollywood production like *Hidden Figures*

GENIUS

HAS

NO RACE

HIDDEN FIGURES

JANUARY 6

PG

FIG. 4 Promotional image for *Hidden Figures*, directed by Theodore Melfi. © 2016 20th Century Fox.

travels in ways that extend far beyond the screen: it circulates as a movie poster, as a trailer, as billboards and banners; as a presence among awards ceremonies; as the subject of reviews, essays, and opinion pieces; as photo spreads in glossy fashion magazines; and as a physical object in movie theater lobbies.[15] In short, *Hidden Figures* is more than a film—it is also a meaningful part of social and political discourse.

As such, it performs a far less ambiguous task: by foregrounding the faces and stories of Black women both real and imagined, the film's cultural, economic, and discursive presence still contributes meaningfully to antiracist and feminist movements.[16] If Black feminism is defined above all by showing the "ways in which racism and sexism are immutably connected,"[17] films that make this connection visible by celebrating the undervalued labor of Black women surely still do important cultural work. We should therefore also acknowledge the fact that their success both reflects and facilitates changing attitudes toward race and gender.

This is where a closer look at Janelle Monáe may contribute to our understanding of Black feminism as a vector traveling across theory, politics, and culture. Where the previous chapter used Afrofuturism as a lens for challenging liberal humanism's normative whiteness, the vector of Black feminism connects the political project of feminism to racialized oppression. In the words of Audre Lorde, "Black feminism is not white feminism in black-face"[18]; rather, it offers a way to engage with feminist struggles without overlooking the fact that race and gender are wholly intertwined and that feminist progress is meaningless if it isn't also at the same time antiracist progress.[19]

This approach opens up the struggle against racial capitalism to a wider variety of perspectives. For in the words of Jennifer C. Nash, there is no such thing as a singular Black feminism: it is always "multiple, myriad, shifting and unfolding."[20] It is a vector that encompasses a wide spectrum, addressing multiple audiences in registers that can strengthen and sustain each other—and where popular culture's power to define and limit us "can also be utilized to undo those restrictions and expose their construction."[21] In this context, Monáe's work as a Black feminist artist and performer is similarly multiple, myriad, shifting, and unfolding.[22] As someone who is a celebrity and public figure with only a limited amount of agency in the culture industry, Monáe's choice to involve herself in a project like *Hidden Figures* obviously contributes to the vectoral movement of Black feminism.

As I argue throughout this book, it is precisely the multiplicity of ener-gies and registers that makes Monáe such a potent force across this cultural and political spectrum. Her performance in this mainstream film strength-ens her own networked identity as a performer and activist. At the same time, these mainstream expressions of Black feminism operate in dialogue with more radical articulations of the same values. Following Nash's call for a conception of Black feminism as an inclusive framework that is open to complex and nuanced readings of race and gender, we must understand Monáe's creative output as a similarly complex network of energies. This chapter therefore examines how Monáe's mainstream expressions of a popu-lar, more "compromised" Black feminism is complemented and strength-ened by other work that directs this vector in more radical directions.

The Matrix of Domination

While there is a wide variety of challenging theoretical work on Black fem-inism, its foundations remain simple. Christine Delphy sums it up succinctly when she offers a simple distinction between the *dominant* and the *oppressed*.[23] This basic dichotomy neatly separates us all into a series of bina-ries based on race, gender, and sexuality. The organization of these divi-sions is, again, deceptively simple: straight white masculinity represents the perfect intersection of domination, occupying dominant positions in every category. This offers every possible advantage both in terms of social status and in freedom of thought and movement:

> The dominant, who think that they are everywhere at home, think that they can choose whatever social position and change it however they please: all possibilities are always open to them. No place and no social position is shut off to them *a priori*. That they don't always make use of them in practice is neither here nor there. What is at issue here is their representation of them-selves as essentially and by definition free, as against those people who— unfortunately for them—are limited by, confined by, and boiled down to their "specificities"; and who are obliged, as in the case of gay women, to put up with the labels stuck on their backs without anyone asking their opinion.[24]

Delphy's materialist feminism emphasizes the political nature of this strug-gle, as these processes of domination are completely grounded in "brute, simple, naked power—not power to be built or power to come, but power that already exists."[25] The struggle of oppressed groups is therefore more than mere resistance to a subjugating force: it is even more powerfully a denial of the dominant group's monopolistic right to name and define *all* groups, including their own.

To give an example, white people in the Netherlands (the country where I grew up and still reside) have traditionally referred to their own ethnicity as *blank*—a Dutch word that carries the same basic meaning and associations as its English equivalent. Consider how the construction of liberal humanism has been grounded in white supremacy that simultaneously disavows this ongoing project at the level of language and ideology: inequality and oppression are continuously reinforced by the very words we use while at the same time proclaiming the universal rights of man. As such, defining the dominant group as *blank* (i.e., devoid of ethnicity) perfectly illustrates how the social power of ubiquitous whiteness is grounded in its invisibility.[26]

As Dutch antiracist activists continued to exert public pressure, the common adjective for whiteness has shifted in recent years from *blank* (blank) to *wit* (white). Predictably, this transition has encountered strong and sometimes violent resistance from white people who object to being identified as such. Their counterarguments run from charges of inaccuracy ("white people aren't *literally* white") to accusations of "reverse racism."[27] This tension illustrates yet again that the "most sinister thing about whiteness is precisely its invisibility, its inscrutability."[28] Or, as Richard Dyer so memorably phrased it, "the equation of being white with being human secures a position of power."[29]

What speaks most plainly across these expressions of resistance is the dominant group's outrage over being renamed by those they dominate. This is, of course, intolerable—not just because it reverses the existing power structure, but because it *exposes the actual process of domination*. This revelation is the greater threat, for it shows how deeply our social order is embedded in gendered and racialized forms of oppression—what Patricia Hill Collins has named the *matrix of domination*.[30] Long before intersectionality became a commonly used term to express the stratified network of hierarchical power, Black feminist theorists have consistently emphasized the interlocking nature of these forms of social dominance.[31] The matrix of domination provides an effective way of articulating racial capitalism's multiplying forms of oppression: a theory of power fundamentally committed to understanding "how sexism, homophobia, racism, and capitalism" constitute interlocking components.[32] Black feminism has been dedicated to exposing and transforming these forms of oppression through creative and scholarly work, political organizing, and social activism.[33]

Like many other Black feminist artists, Janelle Monáe has devoted much of her career to developing counternarratives that challenge and reorganize the existing social hierarchy. Her work counters the matrix of domination through her constant weaving together of creative work and activism, always choosing forms that "reiterate the continuity of art and life."[34] Throughout her work, Monáe has thereby developed what Paul Gilroy calls "rescuing critiques" that mobilize memories of the past while inventing alternative histories that fuel utopian hopes.[35]

Transformationist Black Feminism

Monáe's acting breakthrough in *Hidden Figures* was followed by a variety of roles that expressed different aspects of Black feminist thought. In *Moonlight* (2016), she played a surrogate mother whose unconditional support reminds us that antiracist struggle "is waged not only through spectacles of black protest and excellence but also through intimate forms of black love"[36]; in *Welcome to Marwen* (2018), she played a disabled caregiver and physical therapist who is also a member of an imaginary squad of Nazi-killing Barbie dolls; in *Harriet* (2019), she played Marie Buchanan, a free Black woman in the pre–Civil War South, who assists Harriet Tubman in a fictionalized dramatization of her early years; and in the Gloria Steinem biopic *The Glorias* (2020), she played pioneering Black feminist Dorothy Pittman Hughes, whose tireless activism shifted Steinem's trajectory away from white feminism's "imagined post- or nonracial sisterhood."[37]

This growing filmography contributes directly to the wider dissemination of Black feminism's vectoral movement. In Monáe's own words, she selects these roles by first asking if the role is really "pushing culture forward? . . . How is it helping to elevate artists and black women and black folks and marginalized voices?"[38] Even without authorial control over these productions, this illustrates how the roles she chooses also express an explicitly Black feminist agenda. At the same time, they also provide her with a larger platform to speak out on the many issues that fall within this vector.

One such occasion was her appearance as a presenter at the 2018 Grammy Awards ceremony. Ascending the podium to introduce Kesha—a pop star who famously sued her former producer Dr. Luke for sexual, physical, verbal, and emotional abuse[39]—Janelle Monáe spoke out powerfully about the music industry's rampant sexism:

> Tonight, I am proud to stand in solidarity as not just an artist, but a young woman, with my fellow sisters in this room who make up the music industry—artists, writers, assistants, publicists, CEOs, producers, engineers and women from all sectors of the business. We are also daughters, wives, mothers, sisters and human beings. We come in peace, but we mean business. To those who would dare try and silence us, we offer you two words: *time's up*. We say time's up for pay inequality, discrimination or harassment of any kind, and the abuse of power. It's not just going on in Hollywood, or in Washington, it's right here in our industry as well. And just as we have the power to shape culture, we also have the power to undo the culture that does not serve us well. So, let's work together, women and men, as a united music industry committed to creating more safe work environments, equal pay, and access for all women.[40]

These aren't the words of liberal white feminism seeking access to existing systems of privilege, nor are they an integrationist request for representation within the system as it already exists.[41] Her unambiguous demand for equal rights instead constitutes a *transformationist* approach that foregrounds the fundamental connection between racism and sexism.[42]

Transformationist movements push beyond symbolic representation, which too easily equates media visibility with the material emancipation of oppressed groups.[43] By explicitly connecting her own celebrity as a Black woman with demands for meaningful change, Monáe's speech expresses what Wendy Fraser describes as a *two-dimensional politics of gender*: it unites the dimension of economic distribution with that of cultural recognition.[44] This dual approach acknowledges that "both the gendered character of the political economy and the androcentrism of the cultural order"[45] exist side by side. Both these dimensions need to be addressed together to constitute a feminist politics that integrates recognition with redistribution.[46] Resisting both the separatist and the integrationist strands of patriarchal antiracist movements, transformationist Black feminism seeks "the redistribution of resources and the democratization of state power along more egalitarian lines."[47] Such a world crucially requires the production and distribution of transformative "re-storying" processes that center the experiences of oppressed groups rather than those of the dominant ones.[48] Janelle Monáe made tremendous contributions to this Black feminist world-building through her embrace of transformationist work throughout the *Metropolis* album cycle.

"I'm a Product of the Man": The Dialectic of Oppression and Resistance

A central theme within Black feminism is the idea that gender and race are quite literally produced by racial capitalism's matrix of domination.[49] Monáe has expressed this notion throughout her *Metropolis* cycle in her android alter ego—as evidenced, for instance, in the repeated line "I'm a product of the Man" on the first album's opening track. All three album covers depict Monáe in ways that consistently foreground the constructed nature of race, gender, and sexuality: Cindi Mayweather's half-assembled, uncannily-white endoskeleton on *Metropolis*,[50] her statuesque face bearing the city of Metropolis like an Art Deco crown on *The ArchAndroid*, and her radical multiplicity as a squad of six identical Alpha Platinum 9000 models on *The Electric Lady*. At the same time, Mayweather's shifting roles throughout this saga illustrate how this matrix of domination shapes her identity—not just in the power it has over her, but also by her character's resistance to this power.

Monáe's *Metropolis* cycle thereby both identifies and resists "the racist, heterosexist, patriarchal, capitalist origins of technology and how these have

FIG. 5 *Metropolis: The Chase Suite–Special Edition.* © 2008, Bad Boy Records/Wondaland; *The ArchAndroid.* © 2010, Bad Boy Records/Wondaland; *The Electric Lady.* © 2013, Bad Boy Records/Wondaland.

been used against black women's bodies."[51] This is something she has consistently emphasized in the many interviews about the thinking behind her creative work: "When I'm talking about the android, I'm not talking about an avant-garde art concept or a science-fiction fantasy; I'm talking about the 'other': women, the negroid, the queer, the untouchable, the marginalized, the oppressed."[52] As discussed in the previous chapter, this aspect of her world-building is articulated via Afrofuturism's allegorical juxtaposition of dominant organic humans versus a subaltern class of artificial humans.[53] But her android protagonist also serves as a multifaceted critique of oppressive gender roles and their many intersections with race, class, and sexuality. For while the android can obviously embody a wide variety of social roles and identities, Cindi Mayweather is clearly and quite meaningfully performed by a queer Black woman. Moreover, her lyrics continuously reflect on the specific ways in which her life has been shaped by racial capitalism's matrix of domination—both inside and outside her fictional storyworld.

This extends from the narrative theme of outlawed romance to the principles underlying her character's physical appearance. In response to the persistent objectification and sexualization of young Black women's bodies, Monáe famously adopted a black-and-white tuxedo as her on-stage "uniform," her hair tightly coiffed into an androgynous pompadour.[54] This combination of science fiction and gender-nonconformism has repeatedly invited comparisons to David Bowie and Prince. But a Black woman playing with gender roles has rather different implications than a male celebrity's subversion of masculinity. Indeed, Monáe's withering response to a white male interviewer's suggestion that she was the "lovechild of Fritz Lang and David Bowie" emphasized that a Black woman from Kansas should not be so easily conflated with white male celebrities.[55] White men already occupy a socially dominant position, which gives them more freedom to adopt the roles of oppressed groups without sacrificing their own power or privilege.[56] Defying those norms therefore has rather different implications for gender-nonconforming Black women.

This makes Monáe's android performance in the *Metropolis* cycle a clear illustration of the *dialectic of oppression and resistance* that is central to Black feminist thought.[57] It involves the reciprocal relationship between oppression and resistance, as resistance to oppression generates transformative acts of antiracist activism.[58] This activism has two interlocking dimensions: the first dimension is made up of struggles for group survival within existing social structures.[59] In Hollywood, this dimension is commonly depicted through dramatized histories of racism, like *Amistad* (1997) or *12 Years a Slave* (2015), which focus on representations of Black suffering without also depicting the activism that flows from it. The second dimension responds to this suffering in the form of struggles for institutional transformation, which connect issues that specifically affect Black women with other groups' social agendas.[60] While depictions of these political struggles have been somewhat rare in mainstream popular culture, this second dimension of Black feminist activism is the key to actual transformationist work.

Monáe's *Metropolis* cycle is centrally concerned with this dialectic, consistently mapping out its storyworld through the dynamic relationship between oppression and resistance. Its most profound illustration lies in the series of transformations that Cindi Mayweather undergoes throughout *The ArchAndroid* and *The Electric Lady*—most obviously in her own transition from android-on-the-run to leader of the resistance, but also in the character's lyrical reflections on her constantly shifting identity. The four suites that make up these two albums articulate this productive tension between oppression and activism: Mayweather's romantic relationship with Anthony Greendown is made politically meaningful by the oppressive society that prohibits it. Mayweather's activism therefore follows from this relationship, while at the same time—tragically—impeding it. The resulting movement is wholly dialectical: her political activism flows from her personal life, which is subsequently transformed by this very activism.

The ArchAndroid: "I Can Make a Change"

When Janelle Monáe first established her Afrofuturist storyworld on *Metropolis*, its four-track narrative sequence had left Cindi Mayweather in the limbo of "Cybertronic Purgatory."[61] But the ending of the album's fifth, otherwise nonnarrative track "Sincerely, Jane" returned us to the character once more with a brief spoken coda that constituted an oblique call to action:

57821
It's now time for you to come home, my dear
You've been gone long enough
Thank you
We must come, we must go!

The two albums that make up the remainder of the *Metropolis* cycle to date map out Cindi's response to this call: *The ArchAndroid* traces Cindi Mayweather's emotional journey as she comes to terms with her messianic role as leader of the android rebellion. The 68-minute album is divided into two suites, each preceded by an orchestral overture that announces the key melodic themes, with a staggering variety of styles and genres represented among its eighteen tracks. Both *The ArchAndroid* and *The Electric Lady* are too long and elaborate to discuss track-by-track in this chapter.[62] Instead, I focus on a few key tracks and emotion pictures that most clearly illustrate the complex relationship between Cindi Mayweather's interior life on the one hand, and her snowballing role as a political leader on the other.

This tension is a core component throughout *The ArchAndroid*'s musical and lyrical organization, beginning with the opening track "Dance or Die." The song weaves together the associative wordplay of poet Saul Williams with Monáe's fast-paced rap verses and a rousing double-tracked hook that makes up the chorus. The lyric revolves around the slippery contradictions inherent in the politics of dance.[63] On the one hand, the repeated line "dance or die" positions dance as a form of political resistance ("Focus, trance, wake up, dance!"). But on the other, this resistance is contradicted by the way military marches turn rhythm and movement into an authoritarian form of control ("And if you want to wake the sun / Just keep on marching to the drum"). It makes the song's fundamental contradiction as palpable as it is painful: what if our very forms of resistance are always already implicated in the structures of power they resist?

This dialectical energy permeates the entire album, which is more focused on the internal tensions resulting from Mayweather's conflicting roles than in telling a straightforward story of a *Matrix*-like rebellion. This firstly counters the traditionally male-dominated macho mystique of previous eras' Black civil rights icons.[64] But it also pointedly avoids what Michele Wallace famously described as the myth of the Black superwoman[65]: Cindi may be the messianic ArchAndroid who inspires others to rise up in rebellion, but she remains above all vulnerable, conflicted, and deeply human.[66] To illustrate, while "Dance or Die" establishes the cycle's oppressive society and the androids' semireligious call for a messianic leader, the next track emphasizes the main character's deeply conflicted response. Framed from Cindi's point of view, "Faster" articulates the pressure felt by someone who can never run fast enough to outrun the invisible matrix of domination that surrounds her. For while the politicization of her love affair is what thrust her into her transformationist role of ArchAndroid, this is also what makes her run "faster and faster from your arms."

This contradiction takes even clearer shape as "Faster" segues into the next track, "Locked Inside."[67] This third song's lyric shifts back and forth between vivid descriptions of oppression and meaningful acts of resistance[68]—for instance when she relates poverty and motherhood to racist structures of domination:

> Her children cry
> No food to eat and afraid as flies
> The color black means it's time to die
> And nobody questions why
> Cause they're too scared to stop the Man

Verses like these clearly articulate the many obstacles Black women have disproportionately encountered, as well as the danger inherent in any kind of meaningful resistance to "the Man." This first part of the song thereby vividly reproduces the material reality of the gendered and racialized oppression that produced Black feminism.

Then, just past the song's halfway point, the tempo shifts abruptly. The breathless momentum of the first part gives way to a more measured bridge, the percussion shifting from staccato drums to flowing beats as a meandering bossa nova bass line transforms the track's rhythmic movement. The lyric changes in perfect sync with this musical change, suddenly signaling the transition into Black feminist activism's second dimension with crystal clarity:

> I can make a change
> I can start a fire
> Lord make me love again
> Fill me with desire

These lines are then repeated a second time, after which the two different rhythms and orchestrations are interwoven to form a new harmonic unity for the song's closing verse. The track's final chorus thereby offers a musical and lyrical synthesis of these two interlocking dimensions of Black feminist activism, simultaneously challenging and reinforcing each other: the first dimension's struggle for survival sharpens her understanding of the matrix

FIG. 6 "Tightrope [feat. Big Boi]," emotion picture directed by Wendy Morgan. © 2010, Bad Boy Records/Wondaland.

of domination, which leads directly to the second dimension of the trans-formationist struggle for true liberation.

This dialectical principle can also be observed in *The ArchAndroid*'s emo-tion pictures. The album's lead single was the "vicious, greasy, clattering old-school funk" song "Tightrope,"[69] directed by Wendy Morgan and fea-turing a guest appearance by rapper Big Boi, the Outkast rapper and Monáe's early-career mentor.[70] The video is set in a psychiatric hospital called The Palace of the Dogs—an "otherworldly, timeless place where someone from the future would crisscross with someone from the past."[71] Inside its walls, we see a tuxedo-clad Monáe moving through the hallways with a group of Black fellow inmates. While the emotion picture's opening caption has informed us that "dancing has long been forbidden for its subversive effects on the residents," the group's loosely choreographed movements are framed explicitly as "praxes of rebellious subversions."[72]

The album's liner notes, supposedly authored by a character named Max Stellings, "Vice Chancellor of the Palace of the Dogs Arts Asylum," clarify how to interpret the location in relation to the *Metropolis* cycle and its Afrofuturist storyworld. These notes explain that Monáe is being held in this "state-of-the-art federal facility for mutants, lost geniuses and savants." Stellings's notes state that Janelle Monáe is from the year 2719, that she was "snatched, genoraped and de-existed" in the future, where her genetic code was sold and subsequently used to create an android clone named Cindi

Mayweather before she was forced "into a time tunnel and sent back to our era." Such science-fictional elaboration neatly sutures present-day Monáe to her Afrofuturist doppelgänger, while creating a symbolic portal "through which we might imagine the future of Black feminist intellectual labor in relation to sound."[73] This introduction of abduction, rape, and reproductive theft transform the album tracks into a kind of "revolutionary code, the weapons to fight the ominously titled 'cold war' that human and droid are waging far apart and yet in simultaneity with each other."[74]

"Cold War" is also the name of the sixth track on the album, which was released separately as its second single and provides an especially good example of how this dialectical struggle is translated to other media.[75] Its emotion picture is set in the "black box auditorium in the Palace of the Dogs sanitarium." Unlike its predecessor's playful depiction of collective resistance to institutional power, the video consists of a single unedited take of Monáe in medium close-up, seen removing her robe before lip-syncing the song while looking directly into the camera—as directed, once again, by Wendy Morgan. The performance is initially one of almost robotic perfection: we see Monáe carefully tilting her head up, down, and sideways in perfect sync with the music being played back. But midway through the song, this impressive display of microchoreography is abruptly punctured when the line "I was made to believe there's something wrong with me" triggers an emotional response that unexpectedly interrupts the performance. As we

FIG. 7 "Cold War," emotion picture directed by Wendy Morgan. © 2010, Bad Boy Records/Wondaland.

see her struggling to regain her composure, the sight of a Black woman performing naked before the camera's eye becomes uncomfortably intimate.[76]

The spontaneous outburst of emotion that overwhelms Monáe's performance in the video's second half illustrates the recognition of the jezebel stereotype: a common trope that has historically been used to objectify Black women, justify sexual assault against them, and mark them as sexually deviant.[77] This interaction between subject and camera goes beyond the usual music video conventions, in which performers acknowledge the camera's presence and return its gaze;[78] our automatic expectation of a perfectly synchronized performance is disrupted by the spontaneous eruption of emotional "glitches" that humanize the performer.[79]

Meanwhile, the camera's presence is explicitly incorporated into the frame by having a digital time-code on-screen throughout the video. This reminds us not only that her performance is mediated, but that the technology itself is a nonneutral presence. In her book *Race after Technology*, Ruha Benjamin describes this oppressive institution as the "New Jim Code": a technological framework of ubiquitous surveillance that "allows racist habits and logics to enter through the backdoor of tech design."[80] The "Cold War" emotion picture thereby subtly underlines how surveillance technologies have invisibly strengthened racialized and gendered social hierarchies.[81] Monáe's "radical act of self-exposure" makes these surveillance practices visible, while at the same time offering an "alternative to the subterfuge used by oppressed peoples."[82]

Together, the video's dialectical organization and its explicit evocation of the New Jim Code's surveillance technology ultimately give direction to the track's lyric, with its oft-repeated line "This is a cold war, you better know what you're fighting for." The up-tempo rock anthem's deceptively straightforward lyric again expresses both dimensions of the Black feminist dialectic by juxtaposing the pain and vulnerability of personal survival under racist oppression ("And it hurts my heart / Lord have mercy, ain't it plain to see?") with the struggle to transform the matrix of domination ("All the tribes come and the mighty will crumble / We must brave this night and have faith in love").

Most crucially, the power of this music video's perfectly symmetrical organization hinges on the disruptive potential of the glitch: an apparent malfunction that interrupts the smooth operations of systems of power, "not an aberration but a form of evidence, illuminating underlying flaws in a corrupted system."[83] The transformative potential inherent in *glitch aesthetics* is further developed throughout *The Electric Lady*, the third and (thus far) last album in Monáe's *Metropolis* cycle.

The Electric Lady: "Sound Is Our Weapon"

As a concept album that is simultaneously sequel and prequel, *The Electric Lady* adds new layers to Monáe's world-building, its title a sly feminist nod to Jimi Hendrix's similarly expansive Afrofuturist experiment *Electric Ladyland* (1968).[84] The liner notes, again authored by the character Max Stellings, continue the *Metropolis* cycle's metanarrative by explaining that Monáe has since fled the asylum, after which the recordings that make up this new album mysteriously appeared "in a small elegantly wrapped gift box the day after she left." Stellings writes that he decided to share this music with the world "not only because it contained Cindi's truest autobiographical feelings . . . but also because it seems to contain within its frequencies some sort of mystical battle plan." It thereby makes explicit how these works of sonic Afrofuturism are presented as part of a transformationalist struggle against the matrix of domination.

While the album's structure reproduces *The ArchAndroid*'s organization into two consecutive musical suites, *The Electric Lady* adds a new element by introducing spoken-word skits to the mix. They take the form of live broadcasts from underground radio station 105.5 WDRD (an acronym that evokes the word "droid"), where "your favorite robotic, hypnotic, psychotic" DJ Crash[85] hosts a variety of callers voicing their opinions on Metropolis's "android community" and the rumors circulating about the mythical ArchAndroid. The interludes' clever use of Black radio conventions explicitly codes the androids as Black, the participants' banter reviving Black radio's historical function as "a crucial space for community debate and mobilization."[86]

As the album's opening track "Givin' 'Em What They Love" demonstrates, this third installment in the *Metropolis* cycle finds the character of Cindi substantially transformed. Where *The ArchAndroid* was dedicated to the dialectical struggle between personal desire and public activism, this blistering collaboration with her longtime mentor Prince reintroduces Cindi as a confident leader[87]—a robotic diva with "eyes made of lasers bolder than the truth." Following two verses sung in turn by Monáe and Prince, the second chorus builds to a frenzied musical climax, layering an explosive

FIG. 8 "Q.U.E.E.N. [feat. Erykah Badu]," emotion picture directed by Alan Ferguson. © 2013, Bad Boy Records/Wondaland.

outburst of "Funky Horns" on top of Prince's soaring guitar solo and both singers' ongoing "Background Acrobatics" and "Lead Howls."[88] Finally, an "outro" verse moves the song back from the boisterously general to the intimately personal, ending the song with a brief history of "undercover love" as a string quartet ends the propulsive track on a surprising note of quiet introspection.

This opening anthem leads into a powerful funk hook that jump-starts the album's lead single "Q.U.E.E.N."—a celebration of Black feminist agency featuring a guest performance by iconic Afrofuturist pioneer and Black feminist pop icon Erykah Badu. The song's eyecatching emotion picture, directed by Alan Ferguson,[89] clearly articulated Monáe's growing ambitions as a musician, performer, and activist. It opens with a white woman's voice welcoming us to something called the Living Museum. Visible on a video screen before an emblem that reads "Ministry of Androids— Metropolis," the woman explains that she belongs to a Time Council that is specialized in "capturing rebels who time travel." She goes on to inform us that the museum displays "legendary rebels frozen in suspended animation," and that this particular exhibit is made up of members of Wondaland and their "notorious leader" Janelle Monáe.[90] The museum's strikingly all-white interior resonates with the institutional power of Western archives, and the long history of exhibiting stolen riches—and, in this case, Black people—as objects on display.

The whiteness of the museum space is especially meaningful here. Consider the ways in which the Enlightenment mythology of progress through colonial domination has been accompanied by racist discourses of hygiene and racial "purity."[91] In the visual realm, this has taken shape in the form of hegemonic whiteness and sterility, within which nonwhite, non-Western peoples and artifacts are displayed as exotic icons of imperialist conquest. It is surely no coincidence that the most politically charged scene in *Black Panther* takes place in a similarly all-white museum exhibit. In the scene that introduces the film's charismatic villain Erik "Killmonger" Stevens, this obviously unwelcome Black visitor asks a haughtily white female attendant whether her ancestors paid a fair price when they took these items from their original African owners. Science fiction's "overwhelming Whiteness,"[92] then, is merely one particular way of expressing racial capitalism's colonialist distinction between civilization and savagery.[93]

The clinically oppressive museum environment in "Q.U.E.E.N." builds on our long-standing association with such spaces as manifestations of colonialist and imperialist power.[94] These institutions of power/knowledge reproduce the colonial gaze by maintaining a clear boundary between (white) subject and (Black) object. The emotion picture's decolonial energy dissolves this binary by twisting around its racist logic. Thus, while Monáe and her fellow rebels are initially frozen in place by the power of this colonial gaze,[95] its hold over them is broken by the combination of the track's beat dropping on a memento mori record player and—even more crucially— by the intrusion of a fly that perches briefly on the cup in Monáe's hand. While the fly is only briefly registered in two short close-up shots, the insect's appearance holds tremendous symbolic power as an embodiment of the glitch.[96]

While the musical beat that revives Monáe/Mayweather and her rebels is explicitly associated with rebellion and struggle ("Silence is our enemy. Sound is our weapon"[97]), the fly here represents the subversive glitch that disrupts the system's continued operations: an unwanted intrusion that ruptures the illusion of total control underlying all forms of white supremacy.[98] Just as Monáe's mental breakdown in "Cold War" connects the two dimensions of Black feminist activism, the fly in "Q.U.E.E.N." represents a similar kind of liberating glitch. The emotion picture's central spectacle of objectified Black subjects coming alive—a recurring motif in Monáe's lyrics[99]—before her squad of time-traveling Black rebels joyously decolonize the museum by "freakifying history."[100]

This anticolonialist energy is amplified in the many varieties of black-and-white patterns in the dancers' costumes: when Monáe asks "Will your god accept me in my black and white?" the line clearly references Monáe's iconic tuxedo—her on-stage "work uniform" in homage to her working-class parents. But both that line and the video's dizzying array of black-and-white patterns cleverly visualize the binary hierarchies that distinguish dominant groups from the oppressed. The lyric's constant questioning of habits and behaviors associated with those oppressed groups is pithily underlined by the track's regal Q.U.E.E.N., an acronym that plays on the term's common usage as a form of queer slang.[101] At the same time, the title's acronym is a compendium of marginalized groups: "Q for the queer community, U for the untouchables, E for emigrants, another E for the excommunicated, and N for those labeled as negroid."[102]

All these oppressed identities likewise represent glitches whose very existence inherently disrupt the smooth operation of the matrix of domination, as each in its own way pushes back against the hierarchical binaries that make up white patriarchal power. The emotion picture incorporates this thematic motif with the seemingly endless varieties of black-and-white patterns in costume and set design that stylishly foreground the arbitrary nature of racialization as a *technology of oppression*: a form of domination that we should consider "as a set of technologies that generate patterns of social relations, and these become Black-boxed as natural, inevitable, *automatic*."[103] Understanding race and gender not as "natural" categories but as technologies of control helps us recognize the interests they serve, and what we have to gain once we acknowledge that technology by its very design serves the interests of racial capitalism.[104]

Disruptive glitches have the potential to awaken us to this reality. As an obtrusive error, the glitch "creates a fissure within which new possibilities of being and becoming manifest."[105] Just as P-Funk's Afrofuturist stage shows liberated audiences by creating a funkological space of exception,[106] "Q.U.E.E.N." similarly draws on the concept of the glitch as a way to demolish barriers of race and gender. When guest performer Erykah Badu, appearing in the role of Monáe's "notorious accomplice" Badoula Oblongata, repeats the line "the booty don't lie," her words express the larger truth of a radically inclusive humanity[107]—one from which Black women have been excluded by being labeled sexually deviant.[108] But as Patricia Hill Collins has pointed out, "sexual politics functions smoothly only if sexual nonconformity is kept invisible."[109] Black women making their self-defined identities visible therefore constitutes a political act in and of itself.

As the track segues into its rap outro, we encounter Monáe in a different environment, clad in her trademark tuxedo. The sequence's low-angle framing enhances her presence throughout this sequence, while Monáe's rapid-fire delivery forcefully combines gospel music's call-and-response tradition with the socially conscious hip-hop of Grandmaster Flash and the Furious Five, Public Enemy, and Queen Latifah. Marking the transition with the words "Let's flip it," she launches into a powerful rap flow that sermonizes about Black feminism's dialectical connection between oppression and activism:

> March through the streets cuz I'm willing and I'm able
> Categorize me, I defy every label
> And while you're selling dope, we're gonna keep selling hope
> We rising up now, you gotta deal you gotta cope

Her lyrics call out the exploitative organization of racial capitalism, keeping her "underground working hard for the greedy," while simultaneously reclaiming a rich African history. The revolutionary role of leadership and authority she claims includes icons of Black history that run from ancient Egypt ("Queen Nefertiti") to the modern legacy of Black soul music ("I'm tired of Marvin asking me 'What's Going On?'"). The closing lines "Electric ladies, will you sleep? / Or will you preach?" speak for themselves in their call to join Black feminism's movement to acknowledge, resist, and transform racial capitalism's matrix of domination.[110] Monáe here inscribes her persona with the preacher figure's "natural" masculine authority. Indeed, while male bodies are visible in the background as dancers and band members, all roles of authority and leadership are performed by Black women—with the notable exception of the female representative of white institutional power.

But rather than a simple reversal of this long-standing social hierarchy, Monáe's ambition to "defy every label" expresses the core values of a truly radical Black feminism: her stark refusal to accept categorizations that dominate those who aren't white, straight, or male leads directly to a call to activism. "Q.U.E.E.N." thereby enacts both in its visual organization and in its lyrical structure the dialectic of oppression and resistance that characterizes Black feminist thought: only through the articulation of a wholly self-defined queer Black femininity is she able to call out these structures of social dominance, while embracing the ability to take on the role of preacher/resistance leader.[111]

Having started this chapter with a discussion of Monáe's significant involvement in the project of restoring exceptional Black women to their rightful place in public histories of science and technology, I will end it with a rather different hidden figure at the opposite end of this spectrum. Halfway into *The Electric Lady*'s second suite, Monáe interrupts her Afrofuturist world-building and its elaborate allegorical structures to engage directly with her own era's material reality and even her own biographical history.

"Ghetto Woman" is a track that offers a rare moment of disarmingly personal expression by the famously private celebrity. Like the first album's "Sincerely, Jane," the song falls in the register of socially conscious neosoul[112]—its musical arrangement an obvious homage to 1970s-era Stevie Wonder. Like "Q.U.E.E.N." before it, the track breaks down into two separate sections: an anthemic first half, which follows a traditional verse-chorus-verse-chorus-bridge structure, and an extended rap outro followed by a brief melodic coda. The first part of the song is an ode to working-class Black women and the conditions under which they struggle to survive. The lyric expresses not just solidarity and compassion ("When you cry, don't you know / We're right there crying with you"), but also recognition and valorization ("I see you working night to morning light yet no one cares") that counters the stereotypes proliferating across the media ("Even when the news portrays you less than you could be").

Then, in the track's faster-paced second half, Monáe takes the repeated line "You're the reason I believe in me, for real" as a jumping-off point for a fast-paced rap segment that reflects on her own upbringing in a Black working-class family ("When I was just a baby my momma dropped out of school") and the ways in which her mother's struggle is both extended and transformed in her creative work as a queer Black feminist ("Before the tuxedos and black and white every day / I used to watch my momma get down on her knees and pray"). This illustrates another way in which the dialectic of oppression and resistance yields forms of agency that connect Black women across generations: her memory of her mother's suffering constitutes the grounds upon which her own activism is built. As a striking exception within the album's Afrofuturist framework, "Ghetto Woman" brings home the personal struggle to survive and endure within the matrix of domination where race, gender, and class are inextricably interwoven.

In this chapter, I have traced the vector of Black feminism as it travels across the full spectrum of Janelle Monáe's work. Starting with her high-profile visibility in Hollywood docudrama *Hidden Figures*, we have seen how this kind of liberal pop-feminism exists at one end of a broad spectrum of Black feminist thought. As I have argued, the cultural work done by an aggressively middlebrow mainstream movie transcends the clichés and white saviorism of the film itself—first by foregrounding Black women's previously invisible labor and celebrating their long-omitted histories, and second by giving a prominent media platform to Black women like Monáe who perform these roles and incorporate these energies into their public personas.

This gives public figures like Monáe the kind of media-industrial clout to deliver speeches and performances at high-profile media events, from mainstream awards ceremonies to antiracist protests. But it also amplifies her reach as an artist and musician. Throughout her self-authored musical output, we do indeed see her expressing a more radical and uncompromising Black feminism: across different media, her musical world-building shows a fierce and passionate commitment to social justice, alongside the seemingly boundless ambition to explore new narrative, musical, and visual forms for her activism. At the same time, her work unfailingly emphasizes how vital Black music and creative arts are in giving shape, form, and meaning to the vectoral movement of Black feminism.

3

Vector 3

■■■■■■■■■■■■■■■■■■■■■

Intersectionality

On April 27, 2018, Janelle Monáe released her Black queer manifesto *Dirty Computer* to unanimous critical acclaim and substantial commercial success. Up to that point, she had avoided publicly addressing questions about her sexuality, even though her famously androgynous appearance was widely seen as a rejection of normative gender roles. But at the same time, the main narrative hook for her *Metropolis* cycle had been grounded in an explicitly heterosexual Romeo and Juliet paradigm, set within a futuristic storyworld whose "cy-boys and cyber-girls" still seemed to take the gender binary for granted. So while she had always pushed back against proscribed gender roles, her *Dirty Computer* project marked the moment where Monáe explicitly embraced her own queerness.

This "coming out," as the press and public interpreted it,[1] was more than just the long-awaited acknowledgment of Monáe's self-identified pansexuality.[2] By explicitly rejecting not only white patriarchy but also its heteronormative organization, *Dirty Computer* expressed a sensibility, an identity, and a politics that is fully intersectional. Queerness implies that categories like race, gender, and sexual identity only meaningfully exist relationally within a social system designed to enforce hierarchies of power. Queer liberation can therefore only be achieved by eradicating normative gender roles. Or, as Lola Olufemi expressed it in her book *Feminism, Interrupted*: "The first step to crafting an expansive idea of gender is denaturalising it."[3] Intersectionality's fundamental indebtedness to queer theory therefore lies in its inherent "destabilization and subversion of existing categories."[4] For if radical solidarity is indeed at the heart of feminist practice, this solidarity must be grounded in a rejection of the gender binary.[5]

Monáe wasn't the only famous Black woman to release a politically charged visual album during the Trump era. The following summer, mega-celebrity Beyoncé released a similar production called *Black Is King*. A high-profile celebration of African cultures and Black empowerment by a superstar who is also a self-identified feminist would be momentous under any circumstances. But *Black Is King*'s premiere made an even bigger splash arriving shortly after her decolonial "Apeshit" music video,[6] just as antiracist protests were reaching boiling point and while the COVID-19 pandemic focused attention more than ever on video streaming platforms. The production's Black feminist vibe gave the Disney brand invaluable cultural capital, while resonating with ongoing debates about media visibility, Afrodiasporic representation, and corporate synergy.

But in a summer where tens of thousands of people took to the streets to insist that Black trans lives also do matter,[7] it was disappointing to notice that Beyoncé's corporate-sponsored Afrofuturism seemed to have no place for Black people who are queer, trans, or nonbinary. For while *Black Is King* certainly offers a wealth of imagery that testifies to the African diaspora's cultural richness, Beyoncé's tribute to Afrocentrism was also fatally hampered by its devotion to patriarchal norms. The film's focus is firmly on Queen Bey's heteronormative roles as mother, wife, and daughter, while the endless references to Disney's ecofascist fable *The Lion King* bind it to a universe where androcentrism and heterosexuality constitute an unquestionably "natural" order.[8] Many Black writers therefore criticized the film for validating Black identity through patriarchal monarchies, pointing out that our energy now "should be used for imagining real Black futures where we don't have to participate in capitalism and imperialism to be granted humanity."[9]

While the previous chapter described how a Black feminist vector grounds Monáe's work in interlocking oppressions of race and gender, *Black Is King* illustrates how celebrations of Black femininity can also harbor painful blind spots. Intersectionality has become the dominant framework for addressing the messier, more complex networks of power, privilege, and opportunity that are inclusive of a larger variety of identities—especially those that fall outside Black feminism's most obvious focus on power dynamics surrounding race, gender, and class.[10] As a theoretical framework, research method, and critical social theory,[11] intersectionality provides us with an analytical lens that constitutes "a theoretical, political, and doctrinal effort to do justice to the forms of violence that operate in raced and gendered ways in black women's lives."[12] It therefore gives us new ways of mapping out the organization of social power as an *antisubordination project* that is fully committed to foregrounding the complexities of exclusion.[13]

I therefore use the term "intersectionality" here in the way that Patricia Hill Collins has described: as a form of praxis and critical inquiry that is fully grounded in *relationality*.[14] Extending beyond the key concerns of Black feminism[15]—both for better and, sometimes, for worse[16]—intersectionality asks us to think "beyond familiar race-only or gender-only perspectives in order to take a new look at social problems."[17] This new look adopts what Jennifer C. Nash calls an "ethic of inclusivity" that allows *all* subjects to locate themselves within complex and multidirectional networks of social power.[18]

This combination of conceptual relationality and an ethic of inclusivity has fostered a deep connection between intersectionality and queer theory.[19] The resulting dynamic can help us theorize the complex and messy relationships of power that are organized through intersections of race, gender, class, sexuality, nationality, citizenship, age, (dis)ability, and a range of other categories. This intersectional lens clarifies the networked organization of Janelle Monáe's work across media. Much of this chapter focuses on the intersectional organization of *Dirty Computer* as a complexly networked transmedia text about race, gender, and queerness. But first, I will illustrate this vector's central concept with a brief discussion of the TV series *I May Destroy You*, in which Janelle Monáe's music played a remarkably prominent role.

I May Destroy You

An important way in which Monáe's music travels is via its inclusion in film and television productions. One such show is Michaela Coel's acclaimed limited series *I May Destroy You*, which aired on HBO and BBC One in the summer of 2020. Writer-director Coel plays Arabella, a young Black

FIG. 9 *I May Destroy You*, episode "... It Just Came Up," directed by Michaela Coel.
© 2020, BBC Studios, Warner Bros. Television.

English author struggling to write her second book. In the first episode, a night out clubbing with her friends ends with Arabella being drugged and raped in a public bathroom. As she slowly reconstructs the night's events without reliable memories of her own sexual assault, the series depicts the multiple ways in which Arabella's personal life, career, and social circle are affected by this trauma. The narrative focuses on her struggle to navigate a bewilderingly complex social world defined by the chaotic intersections of race, gender, and sexuality.

Connective social media platforms further complicate these networked identities.[20] We follow Arabella and her friends' increasingly desperate attempts to find meaningful connections in an online world, where social hierarchies are both challenged and reinforced by social media.[21] For instance, Arabella's decision to publicly expose a rapist turns the tables on her sexual abuser when a video of her accusation instantly goes viral. And while her attempt to find solace with a faraway friend via Skype ends in misunderstanding and betrayal, the emotional support she gains from her social media followers quickly fills that void. This is visualized by a floating heart emanating gently from her phone's screen, as the lyrical opening bars of "PYNK"—Janelle Monáe's "celebration of creation, self love, sexuality and pussy power"[22]—summons the episode's end credits.

This moment neatly illustrates Coel's interweaving of connective social media with an intersectional framework: the characters' multiple identities are amplified by the overwhelming scale of their online connections. The series' various subplots all deal with this unstable media landscape, as each character struggles to negotiate the messy realities of the social media age. Through its depiction of the unpredictable interaction between changing social norms and fickle social networks, the show effectively dramatizes how our digital world's networked power relations are shaped by the concept of *reflexive accountability* that lies at intersectionality's core.[23] It thereby shows not only that power relations shape all dialogues, but that accountability is also always reflexive and dialogical.[24]

This is brought into sharp focus in the last episode, which brilliantly demonstrates its multiplying intersections by exploding the idea of simple solutions to irreducibly complex tensions. Arabella's quest for emotional closure as a survivor of sexual assault feeds the viewer's expectation of a particular kind of cathartic release, fueled at least in part by our long pop-cultural tradition of rape-revenge plots. At the same time, this expectation creates a narrative challenge that Arabella faces as a writer within the series: amid the escalating chaos of her personal and professional life, her decision to make her own experience the subject of her new book finds her searching for an appropriate ending. Both as a writer and as a character, she faces the same question: how does one bring a narrative about this kind of trauma to an emotionally satisfying conclusion?

The answer Coel finds lies in the dialogic relationality and radical empathy that are fundamental to intersectionality.[25] Her choice results in an impressive narrative sleight of hand, with the finale giving a series of possible endings rather than a single point of closure. After the previous episode's cliffhanger ending has set up the promise of an encounter between Arabella and her rapist, David, the finale initially follows a path that is familiar from the rape-revenge genre: together with her two closest friends, Arabella enacts a suspenseful and immaculately orchestrated retribution plot. At the bar where she had been assaulted, she lures her rapist back to the bathroom, where they inject him with the same drug he had previously used on Arabella. The three women then track him as he attempts to stumble home over the deserted sidewalks of nocturnal East London.

As Arabella and her friends pursue the oblivious sexual predator, the strident beat of Janelle Monáe's "Dance or Die" erupts on the soundtrack, beginning with Saul Williams's poetic incantation ("Cyborg, android, d-boy, decoy / Water, wisdom, tightrope, vision") while the first verse's rousing hook underlines the importance of this moment ("Oh, these streets are forever"). The camera meanwhile tracks the trio's confident strides as they move together in perfect lockstep. As the scene progresses, the track's volume rises and falls in sync with the women's anxious dialogue ("I don't know, man. . . . Have you done this before?"). The music then comes to an abrupt stop as David stumbles to a halt, turns around, points his finger accusingly at Arabella, and collapses on the pavement.

The three avenging angels proceed to assault the half-conscious rapist in a growing frenzy of physical violence, as the soundtrack shifts from *The ArchAndroid*'s opening track to the album's operatic closing number "BabopbyeYa." A carefully edited selection of moments from this nine-minute track further heightens the theatrical register of Arabella's longed-for moment of violent catharsis. Lines that referred in the context of the album to Cindi Mayweather's doomed romance gather new layers of meaning in this context: the line "Where we first met" accompanies a close-up of David's battered face, turning a lover's bittersweet lament into a recollection of disruptive trauma. Directly thereafter, Arabella punching and kicking the rapist in a frenzied rage runs over Monáe's spoken words "This time I will be unafraid / And violence will not move me," underlining Arabella's focus and determination. Finally, her last blow to his head is accompanied by the line "This time we will stay in our movie"—a line that gives the first clue that what we are watching is the movie version of how this story might end.

As Arabella then drags the battered David onto a bus to take him home with her, the dreamlike cues from *The ArchAndroid*'s orchestral "Suite II Overture" play obtrusively on the soundtrack. Having stuffed his unconscious body under her bed, she turns to the wall where dozens of Post-it notes map out her book's structure. Now that her story has an ending, she triumphantly adds the final Post-it to her wall—only to notice that the literal blood on her own hands has now tainted her victory. Like intersectionality itself, this first ending shows that reflexive accountability works both ways: the fleeting catharsis of violent revenge brings no meaningful closure to her experience, nor does it provide a truly satisfying ending to her narrative. In other words: answering sexual assault with retributive violence resolves neither the problem of unequal power relations nor her residual trauma.

A cut back to Arabella in her courtyard, making plans for the evening, then forms the transition to another ending that turns the tables in a different way. In this second version's nonviolent confrontation, she takes David back to the public bathroom and confronts him verbally with the consequences of his actions. She then takes him home to her apartment, where her kindness and compassion allow him to speak openly about how his violent misogyny is rooted in a fear of women. The suddenly remorseful rapist then breaks down crying. In response, Arabella offers him a forgiving embrace just as the cops burst in to carry him off to prison, while David desperately begs Arabella not to abandon him.

After another return to Arabella contemplating her plans in the courtyard, a third ending then sees dreams, memories, and reality bleeding into each other more profusely. This time, the bar Arabella enters is surrealistically empty. Entering the bathroom, the stalls become windows into Arabella's past: in one of them, she sees her younger self giggling with her high school friends. When she walks back into the club, she seduces David at the bar, while his accomplice awkwardly performs a lap dance for Arabella's friend Terry. After she whispers something inaudible into his ear, David follows Arabella back to the bathroom, where they start kissing. The sequence then cuts to an oddly tender sex scene in her apartment where their roles are reversed in yet another way, as Arabella ends up straddling and penetrating David. Waking up together the next morning, he says he won't leave unless she tells him to. She looks him in the eye as her smile fades, calmly says "Go," and then watches him depart—followed by the battered version of him from the first ending, who crawls out from under her bed and walks out the door.

This final moment of letting go clears the way for a fourth and much shorter ending sequence, in which she abandons her desire to confront her abuser entirely. Arabella now decides to stay at home rather than staking out the club, finding closure instead in the publication of her book and the moments of connection she shares with the friends who shaped her journey. As in the double ending of Janelle Monáe's *Dirty Computer* emotion picture, the series leaves it ambiguous as to whether this last sequence is the "real" ending, whether all these multiple endings merely play out in her mind, or whether the entire sequence makes up a composite ending for her book. But the larger point is that these networked trajectories articulate an understanding of power, identity, and subjectivity that is fundamentally intersectional.

Where Black feminist theory's matrix of domination provided a clear model of top-down hierarchical power,[26] intersectionality is especially useful for mapping out the complexity of these dialogic networks.[27] As the resolution of a series that consistently defied easy answers to the messy issues it addresses, *I May Destroy You* illustrates intersectionality's focus on reflexive accountability, and the ways in which all our dialogues, on social media as in life, are profoundly shaped by power relations.[28]

This is where intersectionality has provided a paradigm change in offering a method, a heuristic, and a social theory that Patricia Hill Collins grounds in four basic premises:

1. Race, class, gender, and similar systems of power are interdependent and mutually construct one another.
2. Intersecting power relations produce complex, interdependent social inequalities of race, class, gender, sexuality, nationality, ability, and age.
3. The social location of individuals and groups within intersecting power relationships shapes their experiences within and perspectives on the social world.
4. Solving social problems within a given local, regional, national, or global context requires intersectional analyses.[29]

The *I May Destroy You* finale illustrates this intersectional approach by being attentive to the multiplicity at play, even in a seemingly straightforward power dynamic between a white male rapist and a Black female survivor. Arabella's quest for closure insistently leads us away from easy answers without in any way diminishing the series's dedication to social justice. Shifting from a Black feminist perspective to the vector of intersectionality therefore emphatically does not imply the adoption of a disingenuous "All Lives Matter" perspective that equivocates irresponsibly about the realities of oppression.[30] But by multiplying the axes along which social power is organized, intersectionality helps us map out a greater variety of subject positions by centering the destabilizing power of queerness.

For this reason, queer theory's dialogic framework makes a great fit for this era in which our identities proliferate across a wide variety of digital platforms. I will address the broader implications of this digital landscape for the (post)human subject in more detail in Vector 4: Posthumanism. But first, I trace this intersectional vector in Janelle Monáe's work through an analysis of her *Dirty Computer* album.

Dirty Computer: Janelle Monáe's Queer Manifesto

As her career developed, Monáe has increasingly embraced a *gender pluralism* that rejects any kind of racial or sexual essentialism,[31] an approach

FIG. 10 *Janelle Monáe: Dirty Computer*, directed by Andrew Donoho and Chuck Light-ning. © 2018 Wondaland Pictures.

that understands gender not as a male/female binary, but as a spectrum that allows for an unlimited variety of roles. While an intersectional lens could certainly be applied to Monáe's earlier work, her output from *Dirty Computer* onward foregrounds the multidirectional approach to iden-tity and social power derived from queer theory—or, more particularly, from the thinking of queer-of-color theorists like José Esteban Muñoz,

Saidiya Hartman, Audre Lorde, and Roderick Ferguson, whose approach to queer identity has been especially mindful of subjects situated outside the white middle class. Only through this dialectical approach can one start moving toward the utopian horizon that intersectionality's paradigm shift has opened up.[32] The dialogic organization of *Dirty Computer* maps out a pathway, which the following section will trace through analyses of its individual tracks.[33]

"Dirty Computer"

The first thing we hear on Janelle Monáe's fourth album is her voice articulating the album's title and grounding concept: "Dirty Computer." The singer thereby beckons us into this world, accompanied by nothing but pop legend Brian Wilson's ethereal harmonizing.[34] The a capella opening verse ends with a smack on the snare drum, after which accompaniment is layered in and bass, guitar, synth, and Monáe's own multitracked vocals are integrated with Wilson's falsetto background chorus. But as *Dirty Computer*'s opening track builds gradually to a mini-crescendo, the overall mood remains stubbornly introspective: the combination of angelic vocals and a lyric that expresses a deeply reflexive self-consciousness ("I'm not that special, I'm broke inside / Crashing down, the bugs are in me") establishes an intersectional foundation from which the rest of the album erupts outward.

As a new guiding metaphor, the concept of the dirty computer has obvious similarities with Monáe's earlier android persona and its obvious associations with racial subjugation. But in its higher degree of abstraction, the dirty computer provides a far more open-ended allegorical framework: as a symbolic surrogate for the human subject, the noun "computer" directs our attention to the brain more than to the body, while the adjective "dirty" evokes racist societal norms about sexual deviance and racial purity.[35] To put it more simply, where the android was the ideal vessel for articulating the vector of Black feminism, the dirty computer's inherent queerness aligns itself perfectly with intersectional thinking.

This intersectional framework emanates from its central figure to the album's elegantly dialogic structure. After the title track introduces the dirty computer's conflicted internal world, the following tracks form a dialogic network of tensions, intersections, and connections. According to Monáe's own thinking, the tightly organized album breaks down into three distinct chapters[36]:

1. *Reckoning*: Tracks 1–6 identify racist, sexist, and homophobic forms of oppression while at the same time voicing fierce resistance to their power.
2. *Celebration*: Tracks 7–10 voice affirmations of pleasure, desire, and "deviant" sexuality in a series of joyous musical celebrations of queerness.
3. *Reclamation*: Tracks 11–14 stage a series of self-reflexive engagements with doubt, fear, and conflict that bestow transformative power on unruly dirty computers.

This thematic progression is strengthened by the many connections that crisscross the album's internal structure. Every track has at least one obvious companion piece: the prelude "Dirty Computer" is answered by "Don't Judge Me," a similarly introspective song that responds to its expression of otherness and exclusion; raucous album opener "Crazy, Classic Life" corresponds structurally, musically, and thematically to the grand finale "Americans"; "Take a Byte" and "Screwed" offer complementary statements of proud sexual "deviance"; the searching instrumental "Jane's Dream" is answered by the spoken-word intermezzo "Stevie's Dream"[37]; the propulsive queer Black radicalism of "Django Jane" segues directly into its mirror image of queer Black sensuality in "PYNK"; the light-hearted Prince tribute "Make Me Feel" is followed by the irrepressible Pharrell Williams collaboration "I Got the Juice"; and the lyrical ode to self-care and body positivity "I Like That" is counterbalanced by the painful vulnerability of "I'm Afraid."

Where the *Metropolis* cycle had been expansive and cerebral, *Dirty Computer* moved in a different direction with a fine-tuned combination of infectious pop hooks, alluring sensuality, and disarming emotional vulnerability. As many critics noted, Monáe now no longer appeared to be hiding behind her android double, instead expressing herself in ways that felt more personal.[38] For instance, where "Cold War" would express broad statements like "I was made to believe there's something wrong with me," the lyrics on *Dirty Computer* specify very precisely how this exclusion derives in large part from her queerness. This key component made the album's tightly knit tapestry not only more personal but also a more direct expression of intersectionality.

"Crazy, Classic Life"

"Crazy, Classic Life" is a bold pop anthem that clearly establishes what is at stake in intersectionality's ethic of inclusivity.[39] Over the track's opening chords, young Black pastor Sean McMillan's powerful voice[40] channels Dr. Martin Luther King Jr. by reciting a modified version of the second paragraph from the Declaration of Independence:

> YOU TOLD US:
>
> We hold these truths to be self-evident,
> That all men and women are created equal,
> That they are endowed by their creator with certain unalienable rights,
> Among these: life, liberty and the ... and the pursuit of happiness.

The universal rights declared in this opening statement first situate the album not within some remote dystopian future, but in the political context of contemporary America. Calling them forth in this way connects Monáe's new musical project explicitly to #BlackLivesMatter and the new global antiracist movement. Then, once the first verse erupts, the multiple expressions of agency and desire ("I don't need a lot of cash / I just wanna break the rules") make the gap between the formal articulation of these basic rights and the ongoing existence of racialized, gendered, and heteronormative oppression starkly visible.

While the clearest distinction here is once again grounded in gender and race, they are joined in this propulsive track by a thoroughly queer sensibility. Expressing the desire for a "crazy, classic life" is not only an act of resistance to heteronormative structures of power: it is also a celebration of transgression that points toward a queer utopian horizon. In the words of the great queer-of-color theorist José Esteban Muñoz, this kind of worldmaking "hinges on the possibility to map a world where one is allowed to cast pictures of utopia and to include such pictures in any map of the social."[41] This definition of queerness as a mode of being foregrounds its power as a *modality of ecstatic time*: by rejecting the restrictions imposed by normative frameworks, queer futurity disrupts the stranglehold that "straight time" continues to exert over us.[42] This utopian horizon is fueled by desire—not only for freedom from oppression but also for the right to enjoy a crazy, classic life of "better sex and more pleasure."[43] Thus, when Monáe sings at the end of the track that she was kicked out for being "too loud" and "too proud," she is claiming an identity in which her Black feminism intersects directly with her commitment to queer futurity.

This intersection is elaborated dramatically in the *Dirty Computer* emotion picture.[44] In the film, "Crazy, Classic Life" makes up the first memory that is played back and deleted by the Memmotron technicians.[45] As the song begins, we first see a succession of close-ups of eleven different faces staring back into the camera—all roughly in Monáe's own age group, and all noticeably diverse in terms of ethnicity and gender expression. As the song's first verse begins, we follow Jane 57821 and her squad of four young Black women driving their futuristic hovercar to an illegal party. There, we see an even greater variety of identities from across the gender spectrum making up various subgroups: "there's Monáe's clique, the young, black, wild, and free girls; there's the David Bowie wannabes; and the punks, complete with studded belts and mohawks."[46] Their presence transforms the space into a utopian enclave of harmony and desire, thereby powerfully communicating the utopian nature of queerness.[47]

In this environment, Jane 57821 meets the two characters who become her shared romantic/sexual partners throughout the rest of the emotion picture: first Ché (Jayson Aaron) and then Zen (Tessa Thompson). The latter is introduced while presiding over a solitary marriage ceremony between two ambiguously gendered women, in a tall white hat and matching outfit that references Alejandro Jodorowsky's transgressive cult film *The Holy Mountain* (1973). Another citational act of "compressed intersectional aesthetics" is visualized in the track's lengthy rap outro,[48] where we witness a queer restaging of Da Vinci's *Last Supper*: a pansexual Black woman in the middle of the table, flanked by two naked androgynous angel figures covered in golden body paint, pictured in the midst of this richly diverse community of gender-nonconforming apostles.

The song ends as the party is abruptly shut down by the violent invasion of a militarized police force, as armed drones and masked storm troopers suddenly descend on the scene. Jane 57821 barely evades capture thanks to Ché's intervention, and she takes both him and Zen by the hand to flee this quickly evaporating utopian moment. We now return once more to the series of close-ups that opened the sequence: the five Black faces from among the eleven we saw at the start are repeated, before a wider shot reveals that they are among the partygoers who have been handcuffed and shackled by the police. This selection subtly illustrates the song's larger point: that punishment is meted out unevenly, and that Black people are disproportionately

FIG. 11 "Crazy, Classic Life," emotion picture directed by Alan Ferguson. © 2018
Wondaland Pictures.

penalized for minor infractions ("Me and you was friends, but to them, we
the opposite / The same mistake, I'm in jail, you on top of shit").

As effective as "Crazy, Classic Life" is in establishing an explicitly queer
perspective, its utopian implications are strengthened by the emotion picture's narrative concept. The key to understanding both intersectionality
and its fundamental grounding in queer theory lies in its utilization of the
open horizon as its most basic paradigm.[49] This means that queer futurity
is neither a state of being nor a destination to be reached: it is a potentiality
that is ignited through gesture, dance, story, song, and encounter—those
ephemeral moments that linger meaningfully as the promise of something
better, something richer, something more beautiful yet to come. In the context of the emotion picture's narrative, the track's utopian power therefore
derives precisely from the fact that it is presented to us only as a memory of
momentary freedom: not as a state of being, but as a fleeting moment of
queer utopian potentiality.

"Take a Byte"/"Screwed"

Throughout *Dirty Computer*, Monáe's "explicit, ecstatic, and self-directed"
queerness[50] provides the crucial component that destabilizes straight time's
binaries while emphasizing the political potential of pleasure and desire. The
next two tracks "Take a Byte" and "Screwed"—connected by the nineteen-
second instrumental "Jane's Dream"—most clearly illustrate this connection
between the album's thematic organization and the queer time of intersectionality's horizon of possibility.[51]

"Take a Byte" is organized around a cheeky bit of wordplay: the phrase "take a bite" has obvious sexual meanings that the lyrical content dislodges from their grounding in straight time. Even within the title, swapping "bite" out with its homonym "byte" connects the album's central dirty computer motif to Eve's original sin, thereby conflating physical sex with the exchange of digital data. The rest of the lyric then invites an unidentified lover to participate in sexual acts that are marked as sinful. This transgression is deliberately coded as queer: the line "Your code is programmed not to love me, but you can't pretend" strengthens the sense that heterosexuality is merely a form of programming. But more importantly, it suggests that this arbitrary and obviously buggy operating system can also be bypassed, infected, or reprogrammed. The dirty computer metaphor therefore helps us understand and articulate two of the central components in queer theory: first, the internalized self-loathing that is the product of widespread homophobia (as the opening track laments, "the bugs are in me"); and second, the liberatory potential that marks the other side of queerness, which ultimately sees gender not as a hardwired essence, but merely as a code that can always be hacked, modified, and updated. "Take a Byte" thereby offers an elegant metaphor for how queer theory has always insisted "that gender and/or sexuality subvert claims to identity."[52]

This dialectical tension within queer theory is articulated with appropriate playfulness in its companion track "Screwed," which paraphrases a famous line that is often attributed to Oscar Wilde about how everything in the world is about sex—except sex, which is about power.[53] The feedback loop created by this circular argument captures the disruptive contradiction that queerness introduces into the hierarchical organization of normative heterosexuality. The song's lyric builds on this by mobilizing the gender hierarchy implicit in sexual language, and the way these words can both strengthen and disrupt the matrix of domination. For instance, the verb "screw" carries both positive and negative meanings depending on its active or passive use. Like most sexual verbs, heterosexual culture links active forms to masculine and therefore positive values, and passive forms to feminine and therefore negative values. Thus, to screw/fuck is coded as desirable, while to *be* screwed/fucked is very clearly not.[54]

In the song, the word "screwed" plays on both of these meanings at once—first by using the passive form's negative connotations by painting a portrait of a world in disarray: "And I, I, I hear the sirens calling / And the bombs are falling in the streets / We're all . . . *screwed!*" These lines draw on the sexist and homophobic associations of being the recipient of sex rather than its (phallic) agent: object, not subject.[55] But then the chorus turns this distinction around, not by taking on the active/masculine role, but by embracing the passive/feminine: "Let's get screwed / I don't care / You fucked the world up, now we'll fuck it all back down." This defiant call to *get screwed* gleefully celebrates the "passive" sexual act without differentiating it clearly from its "active" form—a transformation of phallic power that the song later articulates with the line "we'll put water in your guns."[56] Furthermore, the wordplay that contrasts "fucking the world up" with "fucking it all back down" emphasizes the slippery organization of these signifying systems. Lyrics such as these playfully express the destructive nature of masculine power by queering its androcentric vocabulary.

The song then slows down before ending with a short rap outro that speaks to the many ways in which heteromasculinity dictates feminine and queer expression: when Monáe addresses a "hundred men" policing her body while "blocking equal pay," she underlines how sexism, racism, and homophobia intersect and amplify each other. By the same token, the line "Still in The Matrix eatin' on the blue pills" plays on a range of mutually reinforcing meanings: first, its reference to *The Matrix* calls out the straight men she's addressing as the willing subjects of an artificial reality; second, it reclaims a central symbol from a film made by two trans women from the incels and Men's Rights Activists who turned "red-pilling" into a cultural shorthand for misogynist radicalization; and third, as a sly reference to Viagra—the famous "little blue pill" that props up heteromasculinity's phallic potency in the most literal sense.

Finally, the outro's last line "I'm tired of Hoteps tryna tell me how to feel / For real" underlines the fact that an intersectional framework doesn't organize social groups into neatly hierarchical categories of social power. As a Black vernacular term that found widespread use on the internet, "Hotep" refers to Black men who align themselves with antiracist movements while at the same time endorsing sexist and homophobic attitudes. In the same way that many white radical feminists have struggled tirelessly for white women's rights while excluding Black, trans, and nonbinary women (not to mention sex workers!), Monáe's Hotep reference emphasizes that heteromasculinity is as much a problem as whiteness—and that only an explicitly intersectional feminism offers a progressive way to "fuck it all back down."

Finally, as the outro winds down and the song's groove settles into a repeated partial sample of its recurring lines "Let's get . . ." and "I don't care,"

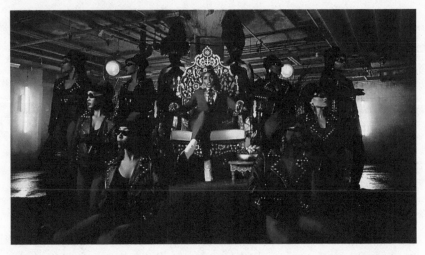

FIG. 12 "Django Jane," emotion picture directed by Andrew Donoho. © 2018 Wondaland Pictures.

the track segues seamlessly into "Django Jane"—a song that makes up another set of companion tracks together with "PYNK," both of which express in different ways the utopian potential of queer futurity.

"Django Jane"/"PYNK"

"Django Jane" was one of the first tracks from *Dirty Computer* to be released as singles several months ahead of the album. In the eye-catching music video directed by Andrew Donoho and Chuck Lightning,[57] Monáe appears alongside a squad of leather-clad Black women in sunglasses, all wearing regal kufi caps as they pose in a variety of similar locations: a carpeted hothouse, a warehouse throne room, and a Moroccan-inspired dinner table, all decorated with intricate West-African design elements. The only full rap track on this or any other Monáe album, "Django Jane" is a showpiece for her skill as an MC that picks up on and further develops the sermonizing persona featured at the end of "Q.U.E.E.N."

The iconography here is awash in the aesthetics of Black radicalism. Monáe's pose, wardrobe, and framing evoke Black Panther iconography—though Huey Newton's iconic wicker chair has been swapped out for a white floral throne, and her immaculate tailored suits resemble a more colorful Nation of Islam uniform.[58] But as in Beyoncé's similarly themed 2016 Super Bowl halftime show, male leadership has been swapped out for what Monáe calls "Black girl magic, y'all can't stand it." Not only does Django Jane's entourage consist only of Black "ungendered" women,[59] but their lyrics and poses effortlessly take on traditionally masculine roles defined by strength, self-reliance, and leadership. From the opening line "Yeah, this is my palace" to her appropriation of gender-swapped pop-culture heroes both Black and white ("And Jane Bond, never Jane Doe / And I Django, never Sambo"), Monáe's "Django Jane" persona is an answer to the previous track's exasperation over "Hoteps telling her how to feel."

As the only full-throated rap track on the album, the "Django Jane" lyric is by far the most expansive on *Dirty Computer*, its high-speed delivery a true cannonade of Black queer feminist pride. Speaking about the track in interviews, Monáe has repeatedly emphasized that it was meant to bolster Black womanhood: "Django Jane is a spirit that will never die. Every black woman—every woman—feels like, 'Well, OK, Django Jane is a part of me.' I don't think it's just me that feels like they're tired, they're upset. Tired of protesting, tired of having to see patriarchy speak all the time. It's like, 'Shut up, get away.' When I wrote these lyrics, it was coming from a place of, if women, if Black women had the mic, what would we wanna say?"[60] The video draws out this defiant energy in explicitly queer ways, giving compelling shape to Black female leadership by performances of gender that casually discard masculinity.

This is more than a matter of costuming, physical poses, or lyrical power. It speaks through the subtle ways in which Monáe's performance in the video dominates not just the frame but also the camera's movements: as she and her squad lean their upper bodies left and right, the camera tilts along with them, its Dutch angles indicating that these Black women's bodies refuse to be objectified by the male gaze.[61] Throughout, Monáe effectively mobilizes the music video star's ability to return our gaze by looking directly into the camera. She uses this power to address the forces of straight masculinity that have marginalized female and queer voices both outside antiracist movements and within them. This is done with a sly sense of humor that complements the character's regal bearing, as when her suggestion to "let the vagina have a monologue" is followed by an overhead shot of her face looking down into a round mirror held over her otherwise naked pubis.

This performance follows through on the thread Monáe established by Cindi Mayweather's transformation from oppressed fugitive to revolutionary leader. It is part of the same intersectional vector that goes beyond the mere visibility of queer Black women in terms of media representation. This

FIG. 13 "Django Jane," emotion picture directed by Andrew Donoho. © 2018 Wondaland Pictures.

is where a track like "Django Jane" marks the convergence of lines established in her film roles, in her concept albums, and in her activism. The raw intensity of her vocal performance together with the video's appropriation of masculinist iconography blends the Black radical tradition with a pop sensibility. This gives her work a lightness of touch that shows her exercising her creative freedom in ways that go beyond the boringly didactic. Above all, it demonstrates that what she has been cultivating throughout her work is the exercise of positive freedom: *freedom to* rather than merely *freedom from*.[62] The track thereby shows her articulating a direction beyond the escape from tyranny, and toward a queer futurity that rewires our current understanding of the real.[63]

This sense of utopian possibility is further heightened within the context of the longer *Dirty Computer* emotion picture. While the three previous musical tracks are presented as meaningful memories in the process of being deleted by the Memmotron technicians, "Django Jane" is experienced as an irregularity: an apparent glitch that confounds the system. Unable to identify the exact nature of the segment extracted from Jane 57821's brain, one of the technicians hesitates before confirming this deletion, wondering aloud whether it is a dream, a memory, or "something else." His indifferent colleague overrides this hesitation and instructs him to discard it. But the scene's ambiguous status as something that is more vision than memory plays directly into the track's expression of queerness as a field of potentiality. Its power emanates from the expression of a symbolic space that allows us to witness entirely "new formations within the present and the future."[64]

The same queer potentiality underlies the following track on the album—which also constitutes the next musical sequence in the emotion picture. Like "Django Jane," director Emma Westenberg's "PYNK" video establishes another utopian oasis within the emotion picture's dystopian landscape.[65] Its intimate celebration of queer Black sexuality is set in an appropriately pink-hued desert outpost where Jane 57821 and Zen consummate their love amid a joyous community of queer Black women. As in the previous video, the sequence is remarkable for the total absence of men: where "Django Jane" refutes the idea that leadership and agency are masculine qualities, "PYNK" demonstrates how queerness liberates sexual desire from phallocentric straight masculinity. But before turning to the video's organization, the meanings expressed in the lyrics deserve some closer attention.

At first glance, the track appears to be a straightforward celebration of feminine sexuality centered on women's genitalia. Indeed, Dutch designer Duran Lantink's eye-catching "vulva pants" featured in the music video and the stage show invite this reading, while the many suggestively incomplete lines in the lyrics point in a similar direction ("Pynk, where it's deepest inside . . . crazy"). But a closer look reveals a radical sexual politics that adds

FIG. 14 "PYNK," emotion picture directed by Emma Westenberg. © 2018 Wondaland Pictures.

another level to the song's already-unusual ode to female genitalia. Those unfinished lines also open the song up to a thoroughly queer understanding of gender. A line like "Pynk, like the inside of your . . . maybe?" is not just being coy by leaving what first seems like a vaginal reference incomplete: the word "maybe" leaves the question whether the woman in question has a vulva pointedly open. Monáe thereby deliberately places a question mark where all too many TERFs would prefer to put an exclamation point.

This reading is strengthened by the observation that the group surrounding Monáe as she performs in her giant labia-shaped pants includes two dancers without them—subtly but unmistakably underlining the notion that femininity isn't proscribed by anatomy. In fact, the lyric and the video both approach the central concept of "PYNK-ness" as a signifier of a female sexuality that is universal rather than particular.[66] The repeated line "Deep inside, we're all just pink" even makes the unambiguous point that masculinity itself is not so much a gender as a means of disguising the more basic truth that *we are all women to begin with*—or, as Andrea Long Chu wrote in her provocation *Females*, that femininity constitutes not a particular identity, but "a universal sex" that is violently rejected by men's pathological drive toward phallocentric dominance.[67]

This performative move further displaces the "natural" dominance of masculinity.[68] Rather than merely reversing the hierarchical relationship between masculinity and femininity, as she appeared to do in "Django Jane," this track's ode to queer femininity presents *all* gender expressions as grounded in desire and identity rather than biology. The video illustrates this by intercutting the footage of dancing Black women with a series of playful inserts of visual metaphors for sex organs and sexual acts: not just vaginal imagery, like close-ups of an oyster and a pink frosted donut with fingers entering its hole, but also the appropriation of phallic signifiers, like a baseball bat hanging down between a woman's legs, and a pink lipstick being extended out from its holder like a tumescent erection.

All this play with gender signifiers opens up a space where denaturalizing gender fosters a more expansive understanding of sexual identity.[69] It aligns Monáe's sexual politics not only with a Black feminist agenda, but with what *Time* magazine referred to in 2014 as the "Transgender Tipping Point"[70]—the moment where trans rights now form the vanguard of the new civil rights movement.[71] Her deliberate scrambling of gender binaries thus highlights how radical white feminism has failed to dismantle the gender system.[72] Once again, this serves as an illustration of the extent to which intersectionality constitutes a necessary corrective to white feminism, offering in its place what Jennifer C. Nash has described as "the kind of ethical, inclusive, and complex feminism required for feminists to revive—and to complete—their political project."[73] Only an intersectional approach brings together race, gender, and sexuality in order to unlock queer futurity's truly utopian potential.

"Americans"

Dirty Computer opens up this inclusive queer futurity through its dialogic structure that branches out across the album. Just as the many paired tracks exist in dialogue with each other, the album and the emotion picture constitute another dialogic network that strengthens and expands the project's intersectional multiplicity. All of this energy is directed toward the scrambling of gender boundaries, seeking liberation through the celebration of transgression.[74] This is first achieved through the variety of gender performances that exist side by side as memories, fantasies, and uncategorizable visions; and second, by ending *Dirty Computer* with the protest song "Americans"—a track that offers potentiality rather than closure.

This tension is established right away in the song's intro: a rhythmic chant that sketches out tensions that are central to racial capitalism in America. This dialectic is then displaced to the personal level as the first full verse articulates a claim of ownership by a member of the social group most associated with "traditional American values." The lines Monáe sings sketch out a straight white male perspective that is grounded in the violent objectification and infantilization of women ("A pretty young thing, she can wear my clothes / But she'll never ever wear my pants").[75] This verse is then followed by a chorus claiming ownership of America through a combination of choice ("I pledge allegiance to the flag") and genealogy ("Learned the words from my mom and dad"). In the second half of the chorus, this self-identification is then transformed into a more combative register, sounding out the warning "Don't try to take my country, I will defend my land," and culminating in the repeated line "I'm not crazy, baby, I'm American."

The second verse then takes the oppositional perspective of a Black woman whose disadvantages under capitalism are both material ("Seventy-nine cent to your dollar") and cultural ("You see my color before my vision"). This second character follows her verse with the exact same chorus, thereby countering the previous voice and contesting its claim of ownership. Both contrasting voices are then followed by a second speech by Rev. Dr. Sean McMillan, whose reading of the Declaration of Independence had opened the album. Where his previous words had stated a general aspirational truth, this second recording expresses the particular ways in which the American right to life, liberty, and the pursuit of happiness seems guaranteed only for the socially dominant group:

> Until women can get equal pay for equal work . . .
> Until same-gender-loving people can be who they are . . .
> Until Black people can come home from a police stop without being
>   shot in the head
> This is not my America

The list of ways in which oppression is shaped by intersecting identities goes on, effectively summarizing how gender, race, sexuality, and class constitute the primary categories of violence and exclusion. But it culminates with a fierce rejection of the inevitability of social injustice, proclaiming the utopian hope that "it's gonna be my America before it's all over."

This short speech powerfully summarizes the deep tensions that characterize America's matrix of domination. As the nation that has presided over racial capitalism's global hegemony, the unfulfilled promise of equal rights is simultaneously critiqued and revived in this infectious track that "bounces to a beat that marries old school Motown with 1980s synth-pop."[76] Simultaneously liberating and rife with internal tension, the defiant speech's closing lines hold out the possibility of a radically different future in which progressive action is able to overcome these tremendous barriers.[77]

As McMillan's sermon nears its climax, the chorus is repeated with the addition of the line "Please sign your name on the dotted line." These words are repeated numerous times as the song winds down, finally ending the track abruptly with one final a capella repetition of that same invitation. Having established racial capitalism's intersecting oppressions throughout the album, as well as queerness's potential to destabilize them, this ending holds out the tantalizing possibility not just of a new and better future, but of a new social contract grounded in freedom from oppression.[78] Signing your name on the dotted line therefore means not just endorsing a queer futurity that is grounded in the album's intersectional framework, but also agreeing to contribute actively to the collective struggle that will make it possible.[79]

What the *Dirty Computer* emotion picture really adds to the album's own intersectional arc is its central focus on the interplay between memories and desire in the construction of identity. Science fiction's familiar convention of political power being exercised through a process of brainwashing and forcible indoctrination here becomes an appropriate Afrofuturist allegory for the violence inflicted by straight time.[80] *Dirty Computer*'s celebration of transgression exposes the truly reactionary nature of compulsory heterosexuality, which finds its ultimate expression in fascist movements.[81] The formal establishment of terms and institutions designed to maintain this norm through fascist ideologies of domination and oppression[82] operate through "acts of homophobic violence and pseudotherapeutic processes of heterosexualisation."[83] In *Dirty Computer*, we see this fascism enacted in the attempted eradication of precisely those memories, fantasies, and desires that express the truly universal reach of queer potentiality.

With its explicit embrace of queerness, Monáe's *Dirty Computer* project meaningfully expanded the scope of her *Metropolis* cycle with a feminism that is more fully intersectional. But again, this approach is not limited to her own musical productions. It is part of a vector that expands across media boundaries into the roles she has chosen to appear in as an actor. I therefore conclude this chapter with a discussion of the second season of the streaming series *Homecoming*, in which Janelle Monáe plays the role of a queer Black woman who finds her identity under attack in remarkably similar ways—but where the intersecting networks of identity and power prove more complicated to navigate.

Homecoming

The first episode opens with a shot of outstretched forest surrounding a lake. As the camera tilts down, we see a dinghy afloat on the water. A close-up reveals a Black woman lying unconscious in the boat, while we hear a woman's voice asking "Hello, are you there?" As she opens her eyes, the character sits up abruptly, thereby knocking a phone off the dinghy's edge into the water. Taking in her surroundings, she notices a man staring at her from the shore. But when she calls out for help, the distant figure turns and runs off.

Once she has gotten her bearings, she finds that her mind is a blank: unaware of who she is or how she got there, the amnesiac tries to piece together her history by going through her wallet and gathering clues that help her retrace her steps. Going by the documents and photos she finds in her motel room, she concludes that she is a military veteran named Jackie, and that she is connected in some way to a senior executive named Audrey at a pharmaceutical company called Geist. She then locates Audrey (played by Vietnamese-American actress Hong Chau), tracks her down to her home, and overhears a phone conversation suggesting that Audrey is involved in a sinister conspiracy, and that things have gotten "fucked up." Trailing Audrey into the Geist corporation headquarters, she finally confronts her during a big company party, where they lock eyes and approach each other across the crowded, balloon-filled space. Then, standing face to face, Audrey grabs her, kisses her on the lips, addresses her as "Alex," and asks her where she's been for so long.

This sequence of events, spread across the first two episodes, introduces us to Janelle Monáe's character in the second season of *Homecoming*, the Amazon Prime series based on a popular fictional podcast. The previous season had starred Julia Roberts as a military psychiatrist on the trail of a sinister cover-up: her therapy sessions with recovering army veterans reveal that they had been involuntary test subjects for a new drug that wipes their memories—an experimental treatment the army hopes will cure soldiers of PTSD. As in *Dirty Computer*, the plot is thus also centered on how the coercive power of straight time operates by eradicating the memories of "deviants."[84]

At first, Monáe's protagonist appears to be the latest victim of the military-pharmaceutical complex's memory-wiping drug. But the flashbacks that follow show that her character isn't at all what she first appeared to be. The first episode after their encounter, entitled "Previously," begins with a black screen over which Monáe's voice speaks the lines, "Okay, let's go back. What happened before then?" While appearing to comment on the show's own chronology, the words in fact introduce us to a strikingly different incarnation of her character. Dressed in an expensive business suit and wearing her long hair down, Alex is first seen interviewing a young white woman who is describing her experience of sexual misconduct in the workplace. The woman's initial determination to hold her abuser accountable is swayed and ultimately defeated by Alex's seemingly empathetic response, as she tells her how filing charges against her own employer had gotten her fired, while her abuser went unpunished. Recounting this narrative in detail while showing what looks like photo evidence, she expertly manages to turn the woman's intentions around.

Her phone conversation in the next scene reveals that she had been hired by the woman's boss to defuse the charges and avoid a scandal. Alex, as this third episode teaches us, is a conflict resolution specialist who is extremely proficient at navigating networks of power through role-playing and manipulation. This extends from her professional work to her personal life, as we see her providing her partner Audrey with detailed instructions on how to leverage the fallout from the previous season's ending to her own advantage. Following Alex's advice, Audrey quickly moves up within the corporation's management, even though the company's founder Leonard Geist (played by Chris Cooper) objects to her ruthless business strategy. As she pushes through her plans to exploit the experimental memory-wiping drug, there turns out to be one remaining loose thread to deal with before her career can truly take off.

This particular loose thread is the character of Walter Cruz, the Black veteran (played by Stephan James) whose therapy sessions with Julia Roberts's character had constituted the previous season's main narrative. Eager to assist her more hesitant partner, Monáe's chameleonic crisis manager quickly steps up and announces that she "will handle this," adding that she has done this kind of thing before. She then swiftly prepares herself to gain Walter's trust by pretending to be a fellow veteran before injecting him with a high dose of the memory drug. This would make him lose all his memories of the Homecoming project, and thereby avoid a looming scandal for the Geist corporation. However, a small error in Alex's performance alerts the justifiably paranoid Walter to her ruse, and he ends up turning the tables and injecting her instead. This is where the narrative finally catches up with the season's opening scene, as Cruz leaves her adrift in the dinghy on the lake where we first encountered her.

While the thematic similarities with *Dirty Computer* are striking, the subtle differences in approach to race, gender, and sexual identity add further to our understanding of intersectionality and its inherently relational mapping of identities.[85] For where the wiping of memories in *Dirty Computer* operates as a metaphor for hierarchical power, its use in *Homecoming* maps out a power structure that is less obviously top-down. While Geist's memory-wiping drug is put to similar use as the NeverMind technology, it isn't presented as a tool for bringing dirty computers in line with a fascist dystopia's matrix of domination. Instead, it operates as a technology of control with a pragmatic value that intersects conveniently with the interests of corporate and governmental organizations.

But this pragmatic value also provides two queer women of color with an opportunity to advance within a social hierarchy that has historically devalued their qualities and ambitions. This illustrates how neoliberalism's atomized competitive framework does allow for individuals to gain positions of power, irrespective of race, gender, and sexuality.[86] But it also shows that the intersecting oppressions of race, gender, class, and sexual identity don't necessarily result in activism. Instead, *Homecoming*'s narrative illustrates how an understanding of the system's inner workings can also make one proficient *within* the competitive individualism that typifies racial capitalism in the neoliberal era.[87]

Monáe's character offers an especially vivid illustration of the complexly networked systems of identity and power that typify both neoliberalism and intersectionality. As the series implies, Alex's lived experience as a queer Black woman has made her performative abilities tremendously adaptable. Her character underlines this aspect by describing her job to Audrey with the two words "I perform"—a talent no doubt developed in response to a hostile social order. At the same time, her identity as a Black woman gives her implicit legitimacy in the eyes of others who are victimized by the social system's oppressive nature. What intersectionality thus helps us see, and what *Homecoming* dramatizes so effectively, is one of intersectionality's key contradictions: namely, that the injustices created by racial capitalism can also provide individuals with tempting opportunities to seek advancement within a system that at the same time oppresses them as a group.

An intersectional approach therefore clarifies how complex intersections of power and identity yield relational social dynamics that are profoundly multidirectional. As a counterpart to Jane 57821, Alex in *Homecoming* does not have her memories erased by a fiendish totalitarian system of control: she receives a dose with which she had attempted to silence someone else who is considered a loose end, a glitch in the matrix, a dirty computer. Her complicity results from her understanding of the system she inhabits and her ability to manipulate the behaviors it produces. As she explains to her partner with tragic cynicism: "Every day I go in to work, I deal with the shittiest of people, the lowest of low behavior. I swim in it. If something were to happen, I know how to protect us." The most interesting thing about this series is therefore its willingness to demonstrate how power is not something that is simply given to certain groups or individuals based on their axes of identity. More accurately, power is something that is *exercised* within a complex, relational, and multidirectional system that produces multiple competing forms of power/knowledge.[88]

This doesn't rob the show of its critical perspective. Like so many other entries in the conspiracy thriller genre, *Homecoming* unwaveringly foregrounds the deep corruption of the military-pharmaceutical complex. Nor does it shy away from depicting the ways in which racism, sexism, and homophobia continue to permeate these institutions and their workspaces. Indeed, many scenes vividly illustrate the obstacles that queer women of color routinely encounter among white colleagues—both men and women—who consistently ignore them or undervalue their achievements. But in depicting these systems of intersecting oppressions, it does decouple them from the various essentialisms that too often underpin our expectations of how these processes play out.

In some ways, *Homecoming* even goes too far in its desire to unseat viewers' expectations regarding the normative organization of hierarchical power. The season's overall story arc ultimately depicts two queer women of color conspiring with a female military general to profit from the unethical exploitation of an experimental and untested memory-altering drug. But their plot is foiled by the Geist corporation's eccentric but conscientious CEO: a white, male, middle-aged billionaire who somewhat implausibly puts ethical principles before profits. A characterization like this feels badly out of place at a time where billionaires continue to amass obscene wealth for their increasingly monopolistic megabusinesses, and figures like Elon Musk and Jeff Bezos present themselves as world-saving philanthropists while their profits go untaxed.

This off-putting misstep aside, the season's ending engineers a fascinating reversal of *Dirty Computer*'s climax. The emotion picture ended with Jane, Ché, and Zen turning the NeverMind apparatus against its operators and fleeing the New Dawn facility as their captors lie unconscious, their own memories presumably erased by the fumes they inhaled. In the same way, *Homecoming* closes with Walter spiking the punch being served at the Geist corporate party with the amnesia-inducing drug. As Alex and Audrey share a brief moment of reckoning before losing all memories of their shared life, the series ends with Walter driving off toward an open horizon, on his way to track down others like him who have undergone the same treatment and awaken them to the reality he has discovered.

Coincidental as this uncanny similarity between these two Monáe-centric narratives may be, these two texts illustrate key elements of intersectionality as a critical social theory *and* a creative method for cultural production. Their focus on the tension between normative social power and queerness foregrounds the ephemerality of gendered performance: the memories, dreams, and desires that constitute subjectivity exist in dialogue with, but are not defined by, our bodies. Monáe's dialogic performances express two very different ways of navigating this complex and relational system of social power: one that refuses to be absorbed by the system, and another that attempts to profit from her understanding of neoliberalism's multidirectional and complexly networked matrix of domination.

While both undergo similarly invasive processes of memory-erasure, Jane 57821's resistance yields two different endings: one in which she is integrated into the existing matrix of power, and one in which the strength of her queer love allows her to overcome the procedure and escape into the open horizon of utopian futurity. *Homecoming*'s more ambiguous ending suggests that her amnesia may perhaps liberate Alex from her mercenary past. A final encounter with Walter even suggests that sharing his experience may have performed a kind of ethical reset toward the predatory role-playing she has accustomed herself to engaging in.[89] In both cases, the hope for lasting change is slender, but incontrovertibly present. And in both cases, the moral compass provided by Black feminist thought is further advanced by intersectionality's networks of multidirectional power, agency, and resistance.

4

Vector 4

∎∎∎∎∎∎∎∎∎∎∎∎∎∎∎∎∎∎∎∎∎∎

Posthumanism

In the 2013 arthouse science fiction/horror hit *Under the Skin*, an alien predator takes the shape of a desirable woman, holding out the prospect of sex to lure straight white men back to her otherworldly hive, where they are processed into food. But as the alien interacts with humans, she develops a desire to become more human herself. Abandoning her mission of harvesting bodies, the creature tries to pass as a human being. But two anatomical differences isolate her from others: she is unable to ingest food, and she has no vulva. Fleeing human society into the woods, she is followed by a man who tries to rape her. In the resulting struggle, he ruptures her white skin to find a smooth, glistening black surface beneath. Appalled, he runs off into the woods. But he returns shortly after to set her body on fire, and the movie ends as she dies alone in the flames.

The alien is played by Scarlett Johansson—an actress who has repeatedly come under fire for her colorblind willingness to play nonwhite characters.[1] Her position typifies the ways in which many white people refuse to "see race," preferring instead to inhabit a postracial fantasy.[2] Many rapturous white critics saw *Under the Skin* as a compelling cinematic reflection on what it means to be human.[3] At the same time, all the representatives of humanity within the film happen to be white. And while critics have been attentive to the film's gender politics[4] and the film's deconstruction of its star's celebrity image,[5] surprisingly few have asked what this movie tells us about Blackness in a world where full humanity remains predicated on whiteness.[6] And yet, these fictional nonhumans also have tremendous potential for exposing the foundational relationship between liberal humanism and whiteness.[7]

Consider the difference between Johansson's unnamed alien and Janelle Monáe's alter ego Cindi Mayweather: in *Under the Skin*, the revelation of black skin underneath her white mask marks her not just as alien, but as fundamentally nonhuman. Contrast this with the *Metropolis: The Chase Suite* album cover, where we see the opposite: a Black woman exposing the white artificial endoskeleton under her skin, signifying that she is neither organically human nor anatomically female. As the prominent display of her serial number 57821 makes clear, she was produced to be an object—not a subject. But of course, we relate to the character of Cindi Mayweather as a fully human being, with desires, fears, talents, doubts, and ambitions.

Monáe's world-building thereby helps us see how Western definitions of "the human" have always been grounded in dehumanizing processes of exclusion: her *Metropolis* cycle used the android figure as a vessel for those who are denied their humanity, while *Dirty Computer* broadened this framework by foregrounding queerness.[8] These interventions place Janelle Monáe's work within the larger vector of *posthumanism*: the philosophical movement that offers a critical correction to liberal humanism.[9] Unlike liberal humanism's singular subject, the posthuman represents "an amalgam, a collection of heterogeneous components, a material-informational entity whose boundaries undergo continuous construction and reconstruction."[10] More than anything else, this means coming to terms with an ethical philosophy that tears down humanism's hierarchical forms of domination and opens itself up to social and political justice.[11]

As the previous chapters have illustrated, the social organization of racial capitalism is defined by a matrix of domination. While this matrix includes race, gender, sexuality, class, age, and ability among its primary axes, this chapter focuses on how liberal definitions of the human have been predicated on the systematic exclusion of Blackness. As Zakiyyah Iman Jackson phrases it in her essential book *Becoming Human*, "Blackness has been central to, rather than excluded from, liberal humanism: the black body is an essential index for the calculation of degree of humanity and the measure of human progress."[12] As a critical vocabulary that evolved out of neomaterialist feminism,[13] posthumanism provides a theoretical lens that helps us see this cultural dynamic of anti-Blackness with alarming clarity.

Janelle Monáe has contributed to this vector through her world-building, performances, and activism. Following the previous chapters' vectoral movements of Afrofuturism, Black feminism, and intersectionality, this chapter foregrounds posthumanism's potential for creative work with the power to express Black consciousness as the radical redefinition of "the representative terms of the human."[14] I do this by connecting elements from the albums and emotion pictures discussed in previous chapters with Monáe's screen roles as an android in the series *Electric Dreams*, as a misfit plastic toy in the animated film *UglyDolls*, and finally, as part of the uncanny processes of doubling we witness in the horror film *Us*.

Electric Dreams: "Autofac"

Casting Janelle Monáe as an android in a dystopian science fiction story seemed almost too much on the nose. While the concept albums in which she inhabited her alter ego Cindi Mayweather hadn't quite made her a household name, her musical career had helped reinvigorate Afrofuturism, and her many interviews invariably focused on her posthuman role-playing. Her use of the android from *Metropolis: The Chase Suite* onward never presented her alter ego as anything but a fully human subject: the whole point of "artificial" Cindi Mayweather's narrative of "star-crossed lovers" is that she is entirely *as human* as her lover Anthony Greendown. Nothing about the way she talks, moves, thinks, or feels distinguishes her from her organic masters. The "android" moniker therefore functions simply and effectively as a metaphorical substitute for the ways in which Black, female, and queer subjects have consistently been denied their humanity.

This substitution is so powerful because race itself has always operated as a technology. As Ruha Benjamin argues in her book *Race after Technology*, this definition helps us understand the material organization of racism as "a set of technologies that generate patterns of social relations," which subsequently become difficult to recognize because of their deep embeddedness in our social and material world.[15] Like technology, race itself is a hybrid category that remains central "to negotiating and establishing historically variable definitions of biology and culture."[16] Thus, Monáe's android double helps foreground how all forms of social oppression—above all, racism—derive not from any essential biological, anatomical, or psychological characteristics. They are purely a manifestation of social power expressed through technology.

It is worth noting here that Monáe positions her own appropriation of the android in relation to her two most obvious cultural touchstones: Fritz Lang's silent epic *Metropolis* (1927) and Ridley Scott's dystopian thriller *Blade Runner* (1982). Both these films are genre classics, both are focused on artificial humans, and both are referenced copiously throughout Monáe's world-building.[17] It is important therefore to briefly summarize these films' Eurofuturist conception of the android, and how they position posthuman bodies within rigidly oppressive societies that privilege whiteness.

Fritz Lang's *Metropolis* established many of the key themes and aesthetics that would continue to define the science fiction film genre. The plot revolves around the mad scientist Rotwang, who creates a female android to manipulate the sprawling city's exploited underclass and rile them up to violent revolution. Just before this evil robot overthrows the existing order, the real woman from whom the robot was cloned appears, and her authentic humanity restores the natural order. This last-minute intervention narrowly averts catastrophe by presenting the nonhuman droid as a threat and the organically human woman as benevolent. In other words, Lang's android represents a malicious technology of deception, whose gendered appearance as a white woman makes this posthuman avatar a convenient instrument of mass manipulation.

Blade Runner, on the other hand, presents its android "Replicants" not merely as basically human (or, as their own mad-scientist creator phrases it, "More human than human is our motto!"). They are emphatically introduced as members of an oppressed class of slaves struggling to survive in a world that marks them as disposable objects. Nominally a detective film in which a gang of criminals is hunted down and killed one by one, *Blade Runner* emphasizes the androids' humanity instead: it registers their meaningful social relationships, it underlines the brutality with which the female Replicants are murdered, and it foregrounds the compassion these supposedly nonhuman subjects feel—both for each other and, most famously in the film's climactic fight, for their organic human counterparts.[18]

But then, these Replicants aren't hunted down and murdered by Harrison Ford's eponymous "blade runner" because they lack human subjectivity. It is because their very existence disrupts the existing social order.[19] Their visible presence constitutes a glitch in the system that must be forcibly erased. This positions the androids in *Blade Runner* as fully posthuman subjects whose anatomical and biological origins are immaterial to their humanity. And while there is something off-putting about the fact these fugitive slaves are played by some of the whitest actors imaginable,[20] the film's (and its sequel's) regrettable obsession with depicting a profoundly racist "demographic dystopia" still leaves intact the film's potential for imagining posthuman subjectivity.[21]

A big part of this resides in the film's most famous plot point: the once-controversial suggestion that android-hunter Rick Deckard is himself unknowingly a Replicant. This now-canonical bit of fan speculation underwrites the posthuman idea that subjectivity isn't defined by anatomy. Rather, it shows that a posthuman world requires a fully *transversal* subjectivity: like intersectionality, posthumanism's understanding of identity is profoundly relational. This extends not just beyond racialized, gendered, and sexual essentialism; it also extends further to an ethics of interdependence between human and nonhuman life.[22] *Blade Runner*'s striking departure from liberal humanism's clear hierarchical binaries has therefore been hugely influential for subsequent depictions of the posthuman in science fiction.[23]

Electric Dreams episode "Autofac" extends this posthuman framework by moving beyond *Blade Runner*'s white-focused and androcentric limits.[24] The episode is set in a postapocalyptic world where a small community struggles to survive the fallout of a nuclear war. Led by resourceful engineer Emily (Juno Temple), the precarious group is threatened by the massive ecological damage that is continuously inflicted by the eponymous Autofac—a fully automated Amazon-like factory that continues to churn out unwanted commodities even though there is no one left to consume them. After capturing a delivery drone, Emily's team manages to get the attention of the zombie corporation's AI management, which sends an envoy in the shape of the android Alice (Janelle Monáe).[25]

The rebels' plan is to reprogram Alice's cyberbrain so they can enter the Autofac and shut down production from the inside. But in the plot's first big reveal, Alice tells Emily that she and her friends aren't really the last human survivors of a nuclear war. Instead, they are androids the Autofac has produced with the specific purpose of consuming its output. But just as the Replicants in *Blade Runner* rebelled against the system that produced them, Emily and her group have "malfunctioned." Not only have they gained subliminal access to the memories of the humans from whom they were

FIG. 15 *Electric Dreams*, episode "Autofac," directed by Peter Horton. © 2018, Channel Four Television Corporation.

cloned, but they also refuse to settle for their dehumanized conditions of existence. As Alice explains to Emily, the rebellious androids are therefore due to be reprogrammed so they can once again serve their intended purpose as obedient consumers of the Autofac's output.

The realization that she isn't organically human could have been as shattering to Alice as it was for Deckard in the final moments of *Blade Runner*.[26] But instead, their exchange leads to the show's final plot twist: Emily had been aware that she was an artificial human all along. Before departing her community with Alice, she had implanted a piece of code in her own electronic brain that brings down the Autofac once she is connected to its mainframe for reprogramming. After she takes down the factory's central computer with this sneaky bit of malware, the episode ends with Emily returning to her community and embracing her lover, a smile of relief and affection playing across her face in close-up before the screen goes to black and the credits roll.

Thus, what could easily have been a despairing tale along the lines of most *Black Mirror* episodes instead yields a counterintuitively upbeat ending of antiessentialist adaptability. The community to which Emily is restored, free at last from the dictatorial reign of consumer capitalism's automated remnants, is obviously posthuman in the most literal sense. But as an allegory about the nature of humanity, "Autofac" is also posthumanist in the theoretical sense. This posthumanism lies in its striking departure from the traditional humanist divide between "authentic" and "artificial" human. It reveals the pathological ways in which liberal humanism has always had to define "Man" as distinct from and therefore superior to categories such as animal, woman, slave, sexual deviant, etc. This is accomplished by short-circuiting liberal humanism's subject/object binary that separates organic from artificial humans. Emily's acceptance of her hybrid identity represents an embrace of the fully posthuman subjectivity it provides. Indeed, the episode's final twist derives from her ability to exploit her posthuman abilities: like Jane 57821, Emily is a dirty computer whose bugs bring down a system designed to control her.

This radical approach challenges racialized and gendered definitions of the human by adopting plasticity as a central feature of the posthuman. By plasticity, I mean a dehumanizing mode of being that has been violently ascribed to Black people throughout history: "Plasticity is a mode of transmogrification whereby the fleshy being of blackness is experimented with as if it were infinitely malleable lexical and biological matter, such that blackness is produced as sub/super/human at once, a form where form shall not hold: potentially 'everything and nothing' at the register of ontology."[27] This plasticity has made Blackness an essential index against which humanity is measured.[28] Regarding racialized and gendered bodies as plastic, animal, artificial, and mutable defines them "as a means of hierarchically delineating sex/gender, reproduction, and states of being more generally."[29] In other words, plasticity constitutes an anti-Black mode that sees their essence as *infinitely mutable*.[30]

Since liberal humanism has been predicated on the abjection of Blackness, its cultural traditions continue to cast Black people's essence as malleable and therefore, paradoxically, as both subhuman and superhuman. This contradiction is elegantly illustrated in the film *Get Out*, in which young Black men are lured into captivity by a young white woman so they can become hosts to aging white liberals' consciousness. The film's speculative horror scenario thereby perfectly captures the way in which Black plasticity unites the superhuman with the subhuman: their white abusers poke and prod their Black victims' "superhuman" bodies, while their Blackness simultaneously casts them as subhuman—mere flesh that can be molded by those whose whiteness marks them as fully human.[31]

As one of the most literal cultural manifestations of posthuman subjectivity, the android has been an ideal figure for symbolic negotiations of the human/inhuman boundary. Tellingly, these narrative expressions of posthumanism have generally avoided race. As noted earlier, *Blade Runner* and its sequel are set in ethnically diverse story-worlds that remain strikingly preoccupied with whiteness. Iconic android and cyborg figures like RoboCop and the Terminator similarly ignore racialized plasticity in their depictions of hybridized posthumans. And narratives that deal with humans who have been cloned as medical resources for wealthy consumers, like *The Island* (2005) and *Never Let Me Go* (2010), only seem able to imagine these forms of inhuman plasticity in relation to white people—even though they represent larger injustices that have historically affected people of color. Therefore, if Blackness has always been rendered through the lexicon of the inhuman,[32] seeking inclusion within privileged categories of the human clearly moves us in the wrong direction.

Science fiction stories that demolish the human/inhuman boundary have far greater potential to open up the liberating horizon of posthumanism's transversal subjectivity. Sadly, most mainstream narratives do so without acknowledging the crucial role that Blackness has played in definitions of the human. In this sense, "Autofac" also constitutes a missed opportunity: the Black android played by Monáe is the representative of normative (white) power, while the rebels are played by a racially mixed but majority-white cast, thereby yet again reproducing liberal humanism's historical dynamic of anti-Blackness.[33]

Xenofeminism: From Androids to Dirty Computers

Gender has been a more productive preoccupation in cultural expressions of posthumanism. Without exception, all robots, androids, and cyborgs in Hollywood pictures have been clearly and explicitly gendered—from the "gynoid" Maria in *Metropolis* and HAL in *2001: A Space Odyssey* (1968) to R2-D2 and C-3PO in the Star Wars universe. While cyborgs and androids mostly served as popular expressions of hypermasculinity in the "hard-bodied" action cinema of the neoconservative 1980s,[34] more recent fantasies have conspicuously revolved around posthuman femininity.

But disappointingly, the artificial women depicted in these narratives typically reiterate the most boring clichés about femininity. Films like *Her* (2013), *Ex Machina* (2014), *Under the Skin*, and *Lucy* (2014) all communicate in one way or another that these posthuman women embody a monstrous form of womanhood that is hostile to men.[35] These films, all written and directed by straight white men, end up regurgitating liberal humanism's deep misogyny, unable to understand femininity as anything but an unknowable void: "a nothing, merely a possible complement to the phallus, which in this patriarchal conception is everything."[36] And while "Autofac" is rare in its willingness to depict posthuman plasticity as something other than a threat, it, too, fails to avoid reproducing liberal humanism's oppressive gender binary. This further illustrates the need for a more radically inclusive feminism.

The Laboria Cuboniks collective's *Xenofeminist Manifesto* is a provocative attempt to reinvigorate a movement that is too often and too easily hijacked by those whose particularist agenda allows no space for nonwhite, trans, or nonbinary voices. Rewording and updating Donna Haraway's "A Cyborg Manifesto" for the digital age,[37] xenofeminism connects her ideas to twenty-first-century debates on racism, transphobia, and climate emergency, its "xeno-" prefix explicitly emphasizing the alien, the weird, the unsettling. As coauthor Helen Hester explains in her book-length follow-up to the manifesto,[38] the movement's goal is to project a new horizon of radical coalitional politics "without the infection of purity."[39]

Such a world can only come into being through the production and distribution of counternarratives that unsettle hierarchical distinctions between human, not-quite-human, and inhuman beings.[40] While Monáe's use of the android has certainly challenged essentialist notions of race and sexuality, the figure's deeply gendered legacy stubbornly persists. We see this in the basic setup for the *Metropolis* cycle and its familiar hetero-romance of "star-crossed lovers." But it also resonates in other aspects of her worldbuilding across these albums, such as the radio interludes on *The Electric Lady* that serve as obvious connection points that map the android/human dynamic onto our own social reality.

For instance, on the interlude track "The Chrome Shoppe," two female "Electrified Beta" androids appear on the show to announce that night's "End-of-the-World Cyber Freak Festival." Both the obvious distinction between the DJ and his guests and their announcement that "Female Alpha Platinums are in for free" reinforce the emphatic way in which the androids' social organization reproduces liberal humanism's gender binary. While such choices foreground one meaningful aspect of the figure's metaphorical organization, they also diminish the cyborg's radical potential for disrupting gender categories. It is almost as if the gender binary operates as a sort of gravity well, irrevocably pulling representations of artificial humans back to the most familiar male/female distinctions.[41]

This is another reason why Monáe's more recent Dirty Computer concept provides a far more versatile model. Where the android has been an effective trope for expressing and critiquing existing oppressions of race and class, the notion that subjectivity constitutes a kind of software (or rather, "wetware") unsettles essentialist gender norms. It invites us to think of the many ways in which gender—like race—operates as a technology that serves the reproduction of heteromasculine social power. But at the same time, it also reminds us that our identities are not hardwired. Our minds function instead like operating systems in constant dialogue with our bodies. As Monáe explained it herself in an interview: "We're CPUs: our brains are uploading, downloading, transmitting, passing back and forth information. And with all computers you got your bugs, you got your viruses. But are those negatives? Positives? Features? Or not? I think it's a conversation I want to have with us as a society, as human beings, about what it means to tell somebody that their existence—[whether] they're queer, minorities, women, poor—makes you have bugs and viruses."[42]

As her words so vividly testify, the concept of the computer as metaphor for human subjectivity opens up a much wider variety of meanings. The term itself derives originally from the devalued forms of work depicted in *Hidden Figures*: a person (a Black woman!) who does computational labor.[43] In this sense, "computer" has always been a gendered and racialized term. But as a form of hardware, the computer has taken up a central role as a "neutral" technology in the digital age.[44] Using the term in this way therefore allows her to revive some of those original meanings of the word while also using it to expand its range beyond particularist conceptions of gender.

When Monáe sings "Your code is programmed not to love me, but you can't pretend,"[45] her lyrics raise fundamental questions about identity, gender, and power that are as central to critical posthumanism as they are to xenofeminism. For if our operating systems have been programmed for us, who has done the coding? If the myth of purity is itself a form of infection, how can we tell the difference between a bug and a feature? If our identity represents a glitch in the system, whose interests does this system truly serve? And if xenofeminism provides a "mutable architecture"[46] that can be endlessly modified to suit our collective as well as our individual needs, how can this strengthen identities that don't automatically conform to traditional gender roles?

As a posthumanist approach to gender,[47] xenofeminism draws on our growing human/technological hybridization to foster the *proliferation of gender differences*: "Let a hundred sexes bloom!"[48] Monáe's Dirty Computer metaphor is the ideal vessel for this gender abolitionism, adopting a non-gendered object as its central metaphor while at the same time short-circuiting the traditional distinction between "bad" artificial bodies and "good" organic humans. Its central conflict is played out instead between the proprietary software that represents white heteropatriarchal power on one hand, and our collective ability to reprogram those codes on the other: what Hester calls "social reproduction against the reproduction of the social as it stands."[49] It thereby provides a radically inclusive feminist framework that embraces the mutational through an "outward-looking solidarity with the alien, the foreign, and the figure of the stranger."[50]

All of this underlines how feminisms that fail to "create a different code" for what it means to be human merely end up reinforcing white heteropatriarchy's proprietary operating system.[51] Just as our computers are constantly undergoing updates and revisions, posthuman subjects are works-in-progress engaged in constant interrogations of the many self-representations and understandings we inherit from our past.[52] Monáe's rebellious androids and Dirty Computers give shape to this new xenofeminist imaginary shaped by posthumanism's transformative potential.

Toy Stories: Posthuman Plasticity in *UglyDolls*

Androids and cyborgs may be pop culture's most obvious posthuman signifiers, but they are hardly the only ones. If we consider how racialization has operated as a set of sociopolitical relations that organize us into full humans, not-quite-humans, and nonhumans,[53] another obvious place where we see this logic at work is in stories about children's toys. An enduring theme within animated films, this cultural obsession stretches back to *Pinocchio* (1940): a foundational film that firmly established Disney's blatantly racist mindset with its "thick Continental ambiance and relentlessly fascist cosmology."[54] Its larger themes about negotiating the blurry boundaries between human subjects, animals, and "transitional" inanimate objects has been a recurring preoccupation for as long as the medium has existed. Disney/Pixar's smash hit *Toy Story* (1995) and its many sequels, spin-offs, and copycats have more recently reshaped this theme for the posthuman era.

In many ways, the computer-animated film *UglyDolls* (2019) is an unremarkable entry in this oddly specific subgenre about toys that come to life. It is a formulaic children's film based on a popular toy brand that opened to indifferent reviews and modest box office returns. But this otherwise generic film makes for a good example of how race and gender are employed in these allegorical fables as the primary axes along which humanity is granted or—more commonly—denied. And in this case, the particular ways in which this film deviates from the genre's default representational logic gesture provocatively toward a more radical posthumanism.

To outline the plot in brief: *UglyDolls* is set in a hidden place called Uglytown, an enclosed community populated by the plush toy line's colorful and idiosyncratic creatures. Moxy (voiced by Kelly Clarkson) dreams of being owned and loved by a child, which inspires her to escape through a hidden portal with a few of her friends. On the other side, they discover that the inhabitants of Uglyville are dolls that have been rejected by a toy factory because they didn't meet its beauty requirements. The Uglies are contrasted with the more acceptable "Pretties," who go through rigorous training at the so-called Institute of Perfection before they are assigned to children. The Pretties' leader Lou (voiced by former child star Nick Jonas) is the chief antagonist in his fascist dedication to maintaining absolute purity among the toys-in-training. Meanwhile, Mandy (voiced by Janelle Monáe) is a bespectacled Black Pretty who ends up championing the Uglies' cause. She helps them integrate the Uglies and Pretties into a single town called Imperfection, ultimately even bringing down the portal that separates the toys' world from the human realm, thereby liberating all the toys from normative categorization.

The film's generic message of self-acceptance is obvious and trite—compatible as it is with liberal multiculturalism's focus on individual self-realization. But the boundaries it maps out between the toy characters' varying degrees of humanity are hugely instructive. As an allegory about how we police the boundaries of the human, *UglyDolls* illustrates how liberal humanism's surrogate–self relation is ultimately shaped by processes of racialization.[55] Since the human subject has always been defined in relation to an opposite, it must constantly identify not-quite-human and nonhuman others that deviate from some arbitrary norm. While many axes of identity can inform this differentiation (gender, sexual identity, ability, age, class), race has historically constituted this boundary's primary demarcation.[56] And this boundary has been policed and enforced through plasticity as a category of domination that embodies an "anti-black mode of the human."[57]

Liberal humanism's resulting anti-Blackness finds expression in the characters, stories, and mythologies that our children grow up with—and the plastic toys that give these ideas material existence. There is no better example than the false neutrality of the yellow LEGO minifigure. While the ways in which ethnicity are represented can vary per licensed brand or franchise,[58] LEGO's overall racial logic is that the yellow minifigure signifies whiteness,[59] while incidental nonwhite characters are differentiated visually by various degrees of color shading.[60] This transparently Eurocentric framework affects many other simplified representations, a similar logic notably affecting the long-running cartoon series *The Simpsons* (1990–present). In the storyworld of *The Simpsons*, yellow denotes whiteness—again—through the *absence* of ethnic markers, while incidental and secondary nonwhite characters (voiced by the all-white cast) stand out by their deviant skin tones and ostentatiously racialized vocal inflections.

LEGO's literal plastic thereby provides a helpful illustration of how these nonhuman avatars operate as racialized assemblages that "clearly demarcate the selected from the dysselected."[61] Considering the seemingly infinite ways in which Blackness has been eradicated from Western cultural and historical records, the plastic yellow whiteness of LEGO and *The Simpsons* implicitly reinforces a worldview in which Black people don't register meaningfully to them as human.[62] By the same token, the LEGO minifigures' basic gender is male, while females appear to constitute "an entirely different species."[63] Any deviation from this norm is explicitly signaled as such: either by differing in color from the brand's generic yellow, or by having two-dimensional cleavage printed on a minifigure's chest.[64]

This basic logic is so ubiquitous that it requires little further comment. We can see different versions of its basic representational logic at work in the *Toy Story* franchise and, more recently, in the hugely popular *The LEGO™ Movie* (2014) and its proliferating sequels and spin-offs.[65] In these similarly themed posthuman parables, the colorful nonhuman surrogates are coded as white, the narrative focus is firmly on the male characters, and heterosexuality is the only available sexual orientation. Liberal humanism's foundational racist, sexist, and homophobic matrix of domination is thereby endlessly reproduced through these children's stories about plastic human surrogates.

Given this asymmetrical playing field, it is easy to see what drew Janelle Monáe to a production like *UglyDolls*. In her own words, the movie "celebrates the weirdos, the outcasts, those who come from marginalized communities"[66] within a narrative in which racialized structures of social difference are playfully but unmistakably overturned. So without exaggerating the extent to which a feature-length toy commercial might be considered politically radical, it is still noticeably removed from genre fare that remains stubbornly colorblind in its representational politics.

What stands out especially is the way in which the Uglies and the Pretties are initially contrasted along the human/not-quite-human/nonhuman spectrum. In most other toy stories, the plastic surrogates clearly share a single category of not-quite-human plasticity: characters like Woody and Buzz operate as transitional objects that help children negotiate the blurry boundary between the symbolic and the real.[67] Notwithstanding Buzz Lightyear's comical misunderstanding about his own ontological status, there never really is any confusion about where they stand as liminal, not-quite-human beings. And while the toys may compete with each other for their owner's attention, an absolute boundary keeps them confined to a single clear category.

But in *UglyDolls*, the difference between the Uglies and Pretties reproduces an emphatically racialized hierarchy within the not-quite-human realm the toys inhabit. And remarkably, the plot's most crucial transformation is not personal, but institutional: Moxy and her fellow Uglytown fugitives discover that the city they live in is a segregated ghetto, which leads them to rebel against their oppressors. So even though both Uglies and Pretties are voiced by Black and white actors, the distinction between them is entirely grounded in the racializing logic of anti-Blackness: not only are the Uglies characterized by the socially dominant group as fundamentally inferior, but they are subsequently segregated and warehoused in ghetto environments where they are effectively imprisoned.

This racial logic is made even clearer when we are introduced to the Pretties, whose slender physique, matching outfits, and blonde-haired, blue-eyed authoritarian leader unsubtly evoke the fascist coordinates of white supremacy. While ethnic diversity does exist among the Pretties, this merely underlines how whiteness represents a category of social power that grants "ownership of the Earth for ever and ever."[68] The obvious tokenism in their limited diversity also shows once more how individual members of ethnic minorities can access the privileges associated with whiteness while leaving the structures of anti-Black subjugation intact—just as Monáe's character in *Homecoming* managed to ascend a hostile social hierarchy.

This often translates to a media logic that Kristen Warner has described as *plastic representation*: a common representational tactic in which diversity means little more than the inclusion of a variety of different bodies without meaningfully addressing the processes of exclusion that give racialization its social power.[69] In recent years, increased diversity in casting has refuted the long-held film industry myth that white movies are "economically superior" to ones with racially diverse casts.[70] But still, this "diversity" too often reproduces the superficial logic of plastic representation.[71] For example, John Boyega being cast as one of the leads in box-office behemoth *Star Wars: The Force Awakens* (2015) may be considered a step up from the franchise's notorious racist legacy. But despite the promotional material's promise of a young Black hero, the film still failed to acknowledge how Blackness is about struggle more than it is about skin color.[72] While media corporations have enthusiastically embraced liberal multiculturalism's desirable rainbow of ethnic identities,[73] plastic representation continues to provide the baseline for Black media visibility. While such films seem to offer positive representations of Black characters, their appearance only provides the "feel of progress" while ceding more ground than it gains for people of color.[74]

But a double logic applies to the way these social allegories relate back to the social organization of anti-Blackness. On one hand, the sentient toys are usually cast in a master–servant relationship that constitutes a warped slavery narrative.[75] This makes their degree of humanity dependent on the degree to which they are favored and (often literally) branded by their masters.[76] But at the same time, characters like Woody, Buzz, and *The LEGO™ Movie*'s hero Emmet Brickowski are coded as white within these realms. Thus, while these movies are grounded in the power dynamics of chattel slavery, they do so in ways that conveniently cleanse it of its abusive and exploitative nature, even making it appear benevolent, with the toy characters uncomfortably close to the myth of the "happy slave."[77] The racialized master–slave relationship instead becomes a surrogate for filial love, thereby doubly mythologizing white patriarchy's most basic social imperative.

This is why *UglyDolls* stands out in its genre as a posthuman allegory that acknowledges the racial logic of exclusion and dehumanization. Unlike other animated toy stories, its narrative presents racialized plasticity as central to its storyworld's organization of power. The Pretties' Institute of Perfection represents the social process of integration into whiteness—not necessarily ethnic whiteness, but whiteness as what Manning Marable

FIG. 16 *UglyDolls*, directed by Kelly Asbury. © 2019, 20th Century Fox.

described as "a power relationship, a statement of authority, a social construct which is perpetuated by systems of privilege, the consolidation of property and status."[78] Its rigid training program points toward the malleability that is fundamental to Blackness as an ontological state outside a definition of the human that "implies whiteness and specifically nonblackness."[79] At the same time, the ethnic diversity among the Pretties emphasizes that the whiteness to which the toys aspire is potentially available to them, as long as they are willing to submit to its social norms.

This multiethnic constitution of the Pretties initially seems like yet another form of plastic representation, just as Monáe's appearance as a plastic Barbie doll in *Welcome to Marwen* gives the film "diversity" without really engaging in questions of race or cultural identity. But in *UglyDolls*, the fact that Mandy—Monáe's Black, bespectacled character—is the first to understand the Uglies' plight effectively turns this around. For not only is this storyworld based on racial segregation that denies one group's humanity by their failure to meet arbitrary social and physical norms. It also finds its narrative resolution in systemic change, as a key Black character is the first among the socially dominant group to recognize the racial organization of her society's organization of power. *UglyDolls* is therefore that rare exception to the rule: an animated toy story that uses its plastic characters' mutability to expose the ways in which anti-Blackness has been grounded in the combination of plasticity and plastic representation.

Posthuman Doubling: *Us*

Plasticity's double logic represents yet another illustration of how different forms of double consciousness pervade representations of Blackness. In many ways, Monáe's performance of her android alter ego represents a kind of double, while *Antebellum* used the figure of the doppelgänger to interrogate the plasticity that slavery inscribed on Black people's bodies.[80] And even though *Antebellum* drew too heavily on the "enactment of black suffering for a shocked and titillated audience,"[81] the gendered and racialized mistreatment of her character's flesh is effectively captured through this central dynamic of doubling.[82] The uncanniness of the literal doppelgänger is therefore an ideal vessel for dramatizing radical posthumanism's liberatory vector.

As a tremendously successful horror hit that preceded *Antebellum*, Jordan Peele's *Us* gave a different shape to the racial logic of posthuman doubling. Where Monáe's character in *Antebellum* appears to inhabit two historical eras simultaneously, the Wilson family in *Us*—first introduced to us while Monáe's *Dirty Computer* track "I Like That" plays on the soundtrack—finds itself hunted by a set of monstrous doubles. These doppelgängers appear as nonhuman copies of the human subjects they seek to destroy. The film's ending reveals that these doubles are clones, created by the military-scientific complex in an attempt to exert massive mind control over the population. After the experiment failed, the clones, or so-called Tethered, were abandoned in underground silos, where they lived out diminished, not-quite-human lives, involuntarily mimicking those of their aboveground counterparts. Their seemingly irrational violence against the Black human protagonists forces us to ask what drives their monstrous behavior, and how the various on-screen characters are defined in terms of their degree of humanity.

Central to understanding the film's posthuman logic is the way it offers an allegorical structure that negotiates the boundaries between the nonhuman, the not-quite-human, and the fully human subject.[83] To unlock this allegorical structure, we must look beyond the film's own explanation of its storyworld, and focus instead on the three central groups of characters that together make up the core characters of this fable: the Wilson family, their Tethered doppelgängers, and the Tyler family—the wealthy white friends with whom they are on vacation. The Wilsons are the first group to be introduced, enjoying the upper middle-class privilege of a family vacation in their privately owned summer house by the shore. Tellingly, the Janelle Monáe song that accompanies this introduction is an anthem of ambiguous self-acceptance, proclaiming the value of self-love in a world that is hostile to Black people in general, and Black women in particular.[84] This track adds meaning to the Wilsons' depiction as a "normal" middle-class family that has gained access to some of the social privileges of whiteness. But as the scene progresses, the family's awkward singalong to hip-hop drug anthem "I Got 5 On It" provides an uncomfortable reminder of how their Blackness still remains associated first and foremost with the criminal, the drug dealer, the abject, and the social death imposed by decades of dehumanization, exploitation, and criminalization.[85]

The family's summer trip is timed to coincide with that of their friends the Tylers, a rich white couple with twin teenage daughters. As the two families spend time on the beach together, the families' social interactions are clearly strained, their verbal exchanges guarded and competitive rather than friendly. While the Wilsons are obviously ill at ease enjoying luxury items, the more affluent Tylers are blind to their own privilege and oblivious to anyone else's discomfort. This lack of consideration translates to both groups' internal family dynamics as well, as the Tylers' dysfunctional and uncaring family clearly contrasts with the Wilsons' more closely knit family unit. But even though the Wilson family is painted in a much less sympathetic light, it is obvious that the Wilsons are also desperately trying "to prove that they belong by living up to the example of people like the Tylers."[86]

The Tylers' condescending sense of entitlement clearly shows how whiteness operates as "a passport to privilege."[87] The Wilsons' ambivalent desire to participate is what triggers the appearance of their doppelgängers: shortly after the two families' awkward interaction, a group of identically clad Tethered arrive on the Tylers' doorstep. The appearance of these monstrous, inhuman doubles firstly serves as an uncanny reminder of how their Blackness remains yoked to the inhuman. Within the context of the film's organization of power and privilege, this narrative move places the Wilson family precisely in the middle of the inhuman/not-quite-human/fully human spectrum, flanked by the monstrous Tethered on one side and the privileged Tylers on the other. Or, to put it differently: while the fully human Tylers are the monsters they are trying to become, their Tethered doubles are representations of the abject ontological Blackness that stubbornly haunts their every step.

After just barely escaping their doubles and seeking refuge with the Tylers, the resulting action is governed by a dizzying series of displacements. The Tylers are swiftly murdered by their own doubles, who are in turn dispatched by the Wilsons. Therefore, while the violent removal of the Tylers may appear to open up a space for the Wilsons to ascend to "full humanity," the transformed social order that emerges instead reveals the true horror inherent in a world governed by racialized hierarchies. The film ends as the Wilsons escape the seaside resort, while millions of unleashed Tethered form an endless "Hands across America" chain—presumably having murdering all their human counterparts. This notorious Reagan-era media event had constituted a public disavowal of a social system grounded in inequality in its most extreme form. The new (non-)human chain thereby transforms a notorious moment of patronizing hypocrisy into a spectacle of what that earlier moment "both reveals and attempts to conceal: not just gross inequality but its widespread acceptance."[88]

As the uncanny entities haunting the Wilsons are faced yet again with a racialized social order in which Blackness remains inextricably tethered to the inhuman, the film emphatically underlines the historical connection between the 1980s' legacy of neoconservative racism and Trump-era white supremacy.[89] Like the ending of Hitchcock's *The Birds* (1963), a narrative that superficially resembles a revolutionary uprising is more accurately read as an unmasking of the horrific moral vacuum at the center of our social order.[90]

The film skillfully dramatizes this tension as the double bind resulting from the choice between the social death of Blackness on the one hand, and the equally horrific "humanity" predicated on whiteness on the other. While the Tethered are initially presented as the film's inhuman antagonists, the threat they represent is first and foremost that of downward social mobility. If we therefore read the central conflict in *Us* as the tension between the Tylers' white privilege and the Wilsons' ambition to be included in a social order governed by whiteness, the intervention of monstrous doppelgängers makes perfect sense.[91] The film's compelling portrait of deep societal racism is one in which only the lure of whiteness appears to offer the promise of full humanity. But every attempt at integration into this monstrous system will inevitably destroy the very thing it promises.

This insurgence in many ways resembles the android revolution in Monáe's *Metropolis* cycle: Adelaide Wilson's doppelgänger Red (also played by Lupita Nyong'o) is the charismatic leader of an oppressed race of artificial humans, just like Monáe's alter ego Cindi Mayweather. But whereas Monáe's android rebellion is unambiguous in its resistance to top-down oppression, the Tethered introduce more difficult questions about posthuman life in what Achille Mbembe has called our *necropolitical* age.[92] The Tethered's ghastly fate symbolizes how racial capitalism's homicidal nature is expressed through the triple loss of social death: "loss of a 'home,' loss of right's over one's body, and loss of political status."[93] As distorted mirror images of privileged American consumers enjoying luxury items and comfortable family vacations, the emergence of the Tethered makes visible the necropolitical death-worlds in which "vast populations are subjected to living conditions that confer upon them the status of the *living dead*."[94]

Peele's previous film *Get Out* used science fiction tropes to dramatize the way in which anti-Blackness is grounded in the plasticity of Black people, who are subsequently perceived as simultaneously sub- and superhuman. In the more ambitious, somewhat messier *Us*, this posthuman framework is expanded to include the deeper ties between race, class, and the ways in which slavery's technologies constituted "not the denial of humanity but the plasticization of humanity."[95] While the film's convoluted world-building raises more questions than the plot can answer, its central concept is remarkably insightful: the Tethered reveal how "plasticization is the fundamental violation of enslavement: not any one particular form of violence—animalization or objectification, for instance—but rather coerced formlessness as a mode of domination and the *Unheimlich* existence that is its result."[96] Their vindictive revolt against those they were forced to mimic is therefore a revolt against a necropolitical world in which Blackness is predicated on alienation, dislocation, and exclusion.[97] In this context, the Tethereds' rebellion embodies liberal humanism's deeper truth that "being categorized as inhuman, or not quite human, is a privileged position from which to undo the assumptions not only of race thinking but of the other systems of domination with which race thinking is linked."[98]

As the ghostly representatives of liberal humanism's deep-seated anti-Blackness, the less-than-human Tethered perform a role similar to Monáe's anachronistic enslavement in *Antebellum*. Both symbolic doubles represent the historical legacy of racial slavery as the historical cauldron in which "the idea of black difference, of blackness, was produced."[99] It is especially meaningful therefore that both Adelaide Wilson in *Us* and Veronica Henley in *Antebellum* are ultimately revealed to be interchangeable with their respective doppelgängers: Adelaide because the final twist reveals that she and her clone traded places long ago, and Veronica because what first appear to be two separate periods turn out to be simultaneous embodiments of Black plasticity. In each case, the explosive confrontation between the two doubles yields a monstrous composite, as both Adelaide and Veronica are forced to descend into a violent rampage that transforms them into the very monsters they abhor.

Both these examples illustrate the true resilience of liberal humanism's racialized hierarchies. They emphasize once more the need for developing a posthuman subjectivity that eradicates the many forms that anti-Blackness can take. From her androids and Dirty Computers to the plastic surrogates of *UglyDolls* and her involvement in horror films like *Antebellum* and *Us*, Janelle Monáe's movement across this vector engages both ends of the posthuman spectrum: portraying allegorical embodiments of posthumanism's radical potential on one end, while revealing the horrific consequences of liberal humanism's moral failures on the other. These cases show above all that liberal humanism's white androcentrism will continue to define this anti-Black social order as long as racial capitalism remains its dominant socioeconomic system. This therefore brings us to the fifth and final vector discussed in this book: *postcapitalism*.

Vector 5

■■■■■■■■■■■■■■■■■■■■■■

Postcapitalism

Look at the reality of your lives: we live in a fake socialist state—one which exists in name only. . . . The media, the tool of the government, reinforces their position by promoting images of women as wives and mothers. We are surrounded by the very images our mothers sought to destroy. Decades of women's work for socialism, for freedom of choice, equality of opportunity is being swept away. Once again, we are being placed outside politics. It isn't only women who have suffered—you know the way this pattern continues—Blacks, Latinos, all ethnic and social groups suffer as the old sex, race, class divisions re-emerge. There can be no true socialism until we are all represented in government.

In the experimental science fiction film *Born in Flames* (1983), feminist film-maker Lizzie Borden imagined a future in which a revolutionary war has transformed the United States into a postcapitalist state. In this strange new world, the white male newscasters who still dominate the media now eagerly sing the praises of America's socialist revolution.

And yet, the society we see in Borden's semidocumentary footage is all too familiar. White patriarchal hierarchies are still maintained, policed, and violently enforced. Broadcast media still serve as the mouthpiece for powerful elites. Women still provide unpaid domestic labor that allows men to dominate professional life. Black people are still oppressed and exploited by a social system grounded in racist hierarchies. And queer folks are still considered deviant, forever falling through the cracks of a heteronormative society that refuses to acknowledge their basic humanity. In short, the movie shows how a postcapitalism that doesn't address the intersecting forms of racialized, gendered, and sexual oppression is ultimately meaningless. For as the Combahee River Collective stated back in 1974, "A socialist revolution that is not also a feminist and antiracist revolution" will never bring about meaningful change.[1]

A central theme in *Born in Flames* is the role that media play in the struggle for social justice. The film focuses on the variety of movements that seek to transform the organization of power through media work. These pirate radio broadcasters, punk musicians, alternative-media editors, and community organizers lack a clear consensus about the most effective tactics for revolutionary struggle. But the film shows how their efforts nevertheless remain unified in the collective power of creative, expressive, and emotional labor. As Magda Szcześniak writes in her brilliant analysis of the film, "Emotional organizing is revealed as a crucial element of the revolutionary process and is carried out through the use of media: music, radio talk, press articles, and even the hijacking of a crystallized image of power—the presidential address."[2]

Both these aspects play directly into the postcapitalist vector that informs Janelle Monáe's creative work across media. As a socially engaged pop artist working within a commercial media landscape, Monáe has had a typically ambivalent relationship to capitalism. On occasion, she has voiced clear criticism: "In our day and age it's capitalism over citizenship, you know, capitalism over how we treat our veterans, how we treat minorities, how we treat women, you know. When is enough enough?"[3] Similarly, she has repeatedly condemned a system that always puts capitalist interests first, warning that its grossly unequal distribution of wealth and privilege could lead to a "real uprising."[4] But even though explicit comments about capitalism have been mostly incidental, Monáe's creative work can help us better identify and understand the closely interwoven relationship between capital and race on the one hand, and the tremendous anticapitalist potential of creative and emotional labor on the other.

As the previous chapters have established, Monáe's work has had a consistent focus on antiracist creative expression. But creative work that engages with antiracist activism also contributes to a larger postcapitalist vector. Either implicitly or explicitly, Afrofuturist and posthumanist critiques remain incomplete if they are not combined with equivalent critiques of the three central drives that have structured racial capitalism: "The first is the constant manufacturing of races, or species (as it happens, *Negroes*); the second is the seeking to calculate and convert everything into exchangeable commodities (law of *generalized exchange relations*); and the third is the attempt to maintain a monopoly over the manufacture of the living as such."[5] The interlocking nature of these three drives again clarifies the foundational relationship between racism and capitalism. Antiracist activism therefore also opens up a space for creative work that contributes to a growing postcapitalist imaginary.

This final chapter examines how the various strands of Monáe's work across a constellation of media texts bring together key elements that make up our contemporary world of capitalism-in-crisis, while at the same time exploring Black utopian horizons that open up beyond the harsh limitations of racial capitalism. As in chapter 4, I trace this vector as it runs from Monáe's own creative work across other works and artists with which she has been more tangentially involved—such as the films *David Byrne's American Utopia* (2020) and *Sorry to Bother You* (2018).

While desire is among the key thematic elements in Monáe's transformative world-building, it is specifically Black queer desire that provides a "meaningfully political horizon of social transformation."[6] In some of her most powerful work, the liberating desire for sex and pleasure strengthens the collective need for a better, freer world: tracks like "PYNK" and "Crazy, Classic Life," for instance, fully embrace queerness as a modality of ecstatic time that destabilizes capitalism's normative straight time.[7] This desire is translated to powerful expressions of revolutionary love in the short spoken-word track "Stevie's Dream," which harnesses the anticapitalist implications of radical love. By the same token, protest songs like "Hell You

Talmbout" and "Turntables," which bookend this chapter, build further on the Black queer futurity of her fictional world-making to contribute to the civic imagination that informs this postcapitalist vector.[8]

"Hell You Talmbout": *David Byrne's American Utopia*

Toward the end of director Spike Lee's filmed version of stage show *American Utopia*, David Byrne explains on stage how he approached Janelle Monáe with a request to perform her track "Hell You Talmbout." Describing himself as "a white man of a certain age," he says he wanted to get her personal assurance that it was okay for him to perform this protest song by a young queer Black woman. She quickly gave him her blessing, and it became the musical climax that ended his shows. In Byrne's own words, her protest song provided an appropriate reminder of the "reality of the times we live in."[9] At the same time, his carefully phrased reflection brings home a key insight into what it means for a white male celebrity like himself to be a meaningful ally: "I've learned that we have a poison within us, all of us, and I think it's important to realize that I'm not immune to it. None of us are. And then we have to work through it and try and reject this poison, and we have to get it out of our bodies, but you can't just will it to go away. It's work. And it sometimes takes a long time. It can maybe take a whole lifetime."[10] An early version of the song had first appeared as a bonus track on a limited edition CD of *The Electric Lady*. Shortly thereafter, a longer, collaborative recording was released via the music-sharing platform SoundCloud, credited to the Wondaland Records collective "featuring Janelle Monáe, Deep Cotton, St. Beauty, Jidenna, Roman GianArthur, and George 2.0."[11] This collaborative version reduced the track's orchestration to a drum roll, the chorus consisting of nothing but the repeated phrase "Hell You Talmbout" (a conflation of the phrase "What the hell are you talking about?"),[12] while the verses are made up of a seemingly endless list of Black victims of lethal racist violence, followed by the call "Say his/her name!"

It is a song that Monáe has performed at many protests, often standing alongside the parents of victims whose names are being called out. As a keenly focused expression of outrage over institutional racist violence, the song draws on the power of Black gospel music and its central call-and-response principle.[13] At the same time, the bare-bones instrumentation and simple harmonies build on folk music's long tradition of protest songs as an expression of collective outrage. The combination results in a shared experience that moves the emphasis in the performance from the individual to the group: "a process that draws on the experience and insights of the entire community"[14] to overcome divisions that stand in the way of meaningful solidarity.

The song's lyrics have a powerful simplicity that is neither patronizing nor didactic, exactly like the phrase Black Lives Matter. Keeanga-Yamahtta Taylor explains this in her book on the Black liberation movement: "The brilliance of the slogan 'Black Lives Matter' is its ability to articulate the dehumanizing aspects of anti-Black racism in the United States. The long-term strength of the movement will depend on its ability to reach large numbers of people by connecting the issue of police violence to the other ways that Black people are oppressed."[15] Monáe's protest song powerfully calls out racial capitalism's intersecting oppressions in that very register of musical and lyrical simplicity. At the same time, the collective nature of its call-and-response performance helps break down the barriers that reinforce racial capitalism's hierarchical frameworks of competitive individualism.

This same energy courses through Spike Lee's film. It captures a stage show that combines tracks from David Byrne's 2018 album *American Uto-pia* with a collection of songs that span his long career as a songwriter and performer. The album and the tour it spawned were part of a larger initiative called "Reasons to Be Cheerful"—an elaborate transnational art project designed to fight despair in dark times. Its website cheerily describes the initiatives it facilitates, funds, and curates as "medicine for global mental health. Take two weekly or as many as needed." But the shapes these projects ultimately take is more stealthily subversive than these sweet but aggressively inoffensive phrases suggest. This is especially true for Spike Lee's film version of its flagship Broadway production.

As a stage show and a film, *David Byrne's American Utopia* departs subtly but dramatically from the liberal multiculturalism that props up racial capitalism while superficially endorsing a cultural agenda of social progress.[16] Such plastic diversity can only be countered by intersectionality, which operates in the first place as an antisubordination project that is fully committed to exposing and countering exclusion and its many harmful effects.[17] The show translates this intersectionality to a dynamic and fluid depiction of joyous and rebellious human connectivity—an organizing principle that *Time* magazine's review described as "so glaringly simple that it's radical."[18]

FIG. 17 *David Byrne's American Utopia*, directed by Spike Lee. © 2020, 40 Acres and a Mule Filmworks.

One way in which the stage show does this is through its deceptively simple stagecraft and design. Reflecting in many ways on the deconstructionist ethic of his classic concert film *Stop Making Sense* (1984), Byrne and his band of singers, dancers, and musicians appear on stage within a wholly unadorned square space. Silver bead curtains surround the group on three sides, creating sheer surfaces from which they can materialize as performers, while none of the usual static paraphernalia—wires, mic stands, drum kits, amplifiers—impose clear markers of roles and identities. Instead, the bodies on the stage engage in a constant performative interplay, swapping out instruments and roles freely. All are barefoot, dressed in identical space-gray jackets and slacks—the striking homogeneity of their gender-neutral outfits closer to uniforms than business suits that underline the band's diverse identities. The rich variety of hairstyles, make-up (or lack thereof), skin tones, and age groups is even more noticeable on film than it is on stage, as Lee's dynamic use of close-ups emphasizes the group's unified heterogeneity.

One of the most striking figures among them is lead dancer Chris Giarno, who combines a mustache and close-cropped ginger hair with distinctive eye shadow and bright red lipstick—a visually arresting combination of gender signifiers that he wears in order to represent himself to the audience as a queer person who is also a drag queen.[19] Presenting himself in this way, as a queer performer within a diverse ensemble, emphasizes the deep connection between performance and what Roderick Ferguson calls "a multi-vocal queer politics."[20] Reflecting on ending their shows with Monáe's "Hell You Talmbout," Giarno emphasizes the political nature of these performances, and how its call-and-response structure creates "a kind of immediate accountability" by challenging the audience to involve themselves in this struggle.[21]

It is also a strategy that invites a majority-white Broadway audience to reflect on its own complicity in this organization of power. This is where Lee's film stands apart from the live show it documents: by staging its final number "Road to Nowhere" as an encore in which the musicians perform their last song while moving through the audience, the contrast between the young, diverse, flamboyant players and the largely white, middle-aged, gender-conforming audience is stark. It signals subtly but incontrovertibly that attending an overpriced Broadway performance like this is a privilege for a wealthy elite whose toothless white liberalism truly does represent a political and ideological road to nowhere.

In this moment, the intersectional group's immersive performance clears a conceptual path toward a properly utopian horizon. In doing so, Byrne and his troupe of uniformed conscripts embody the spirit of Fredric Jameson's similarly titled essay "An American Utopia." In this controversial provocation, the eminent Marxist scandalously suggests universal military conscription as a political strategy for postcapitalist left-wing mobilization. He argues that the American military is the only existing government institution that provides free access to healthcare and higher education. At the same time, army conscription has the potential of flattening out class divisions by incorporating them into a radically different social structure. In Jameson's modest proposal, such a transformation would cause capitalism's lingering social, cultural, and institutional remainders to wither away, making way for a properly utopian postcapitalism that is centered on the collective rather than the individual.[22]

Of course, Jameson's counterintuitive provocation too easily sidesteps the rigid formal hierarchies that have typified most if not all military institutions, and which strengthen rather than diminish racial capitalism's top-down organization.[23] If anything, these hierarchical divisions have increased capitalism's fascist tendencies by providing "the means for the ascent to and preservation of power for elitists."[24] In other words, it is pretty hard to imagine mandatory universal conscription actually transforming the American army into a force that would necessarily bring about a more equitable postcapitalist society.[25] But his thought experiment does help-fully reveal our culture's deep-seated fear of the collective, which the cultural logic of racial capitalism has conditioned us to see as an existential threat to liberal humanism's precious individualism.[26]

Even if Jameson's utopian imagination of a *literal* universal army is dif-ficult to parse in our current political moment, the way it helps us contem-plate the limits we place on our own thinking can shape our understanding of cultural texts, and the way they contribute to our civic imagination.[27] If we consider therefore how the uniforms in *American Utopia* accomplish a similar goal of utopian collectivity, Jameson's intervention makes more sense at the representational level. The performers' uniformed heterogeneity yields a collective that is united through nonhierarchical bonds of solidarity: nei-ther the "particularity that lurks beneath the universalist claims of the Enlightenment project,"[28] nor any one of the other particularities that can stand in the way of progressive alliances. For while Byrne indisputably remains the group's (straight, white, middle-aged) front man and lead singer, the show's staging consistently emphasizes the collaborative nature of a per-formance that is otherwise strikingly nonhierarchical.

Without stable visual demarcations of fixed roles on the stage, the musi-cians constantly swap out instruments, their flexible and joyous interactions demonstrating the collaborative creative work of mutually reinforcing talents. As the uniformed collective demonstrates in practice on stage, our best strategy for moving beyond racial capitalism's matrix of domination is by recognizing the intersectional nature of these particularities: "Although each has its own distinctive forms and characteristics, all are rooted in, and reinforced by, one and the same social system. It is by naming that system as capitalism, and by joining together to fight against it, that we can best overcome the divisions among us that capital cultivates—divisions of cul-ture, race, ethnicity, ability, sexuality, and gender."[29] While the group pre-sents a united and harmonious front together on stage, the crucial role their climactic performance of "Hell You Talmbout" plays in the show further illustrates how antiracism is a crucial factor that unifies these diverse voices. In this sense, the song's militaristic drum roll and repeated command to "Say his/her name!" enacts a symbolic conscription into this provisional anticapitalist army, thereby transforming the entire space into a rebellious collective—if only briefly.

This tension between the power of uniformity and diversity is easy to identify throughout Monáe's own creative work, most particularly in the musical tracks and music videos that return us one last time to her *Metropolis* cycle. The next sections of this chapter therefore examine how Monáe has drawn on the ambiguous notion of the revolutionary army in her own world-building, and how her work across media has embraced the dialectical tension between love and anger that is central to postcapitalist world-building.

The Many Moons of Black Utopia

The first and only music video from Monáe's breakthrough EP *Metropolis: The Chase Suite* hardly qualified as a breakout hit. But her science-fictional imagination was so striking, her world-building so audacious, and her abundant talent so obvious that it made those paying attention perk up. Science fiction author N.K. Jemisin was instantly smitten. During Black History Month, she responded to the "Many Moons" emotion picture in a giddy article titled "How Long 'Til Black Future Month? The Toxins of Speculative Fiction, and the Antidote that is Janelle Monáe." The essay reflects bitterly on the overall whiteness of fantastic fiction, and the rare burst of color that Monáe's emotion picture breathes into it: "I'm watching Janelle Monáe's 'Many Moons' short film, which a friend has emailed to me with a cryptic 'HOLY SHIT WATCH THIS' note. It's a scene of dystopian decadence supported by android labor: there's a slave auction going on, but it looks more like a fashion show. While her fellow commodities prance about on display, Janelle Monáe's character is blowing up the stage. An audience of the hoi polloi screams and jiggles all around her. It's completely nonsensical, and completely entrancing."[30] Remarking first on Monáe's striking "genderqueerness" even at this early stage of her career, Jemisin goes on to note the "army of androids" that figures so prominently in the video. Some shots of identical androids certainly do suggest the idea of a uniformed regiment. But as in *American Utopia*, there is a strong focus throughout the video on the ways in which these androids are also different from each other.

The emotion picture's setting is a futuristic hybrid of rock concert, fashion show, and slave auction—a combination of elements as uncanny as it is unsettling. On-screen captions identify a variety of eccentric characters in the audience, while "Golden Hostess Lady Maxxa" introduces Cindi Mayweather as the original prototype of the Alpha Platinum 9000 android line. Quickly changing her skin color from plastic-white to organic-Black with

FIG. 18 "Many Moons—Official Short Film," emotion picture directed by Alan Ferguson. © 2008, Bad Boy Records/Wondaland.

the push of a button, Mayweather ascends the stage with her band while the crowd (composed predominantly of young women) goes wild. As her performance of the musical track continues, several different versions of the same android model, each with their unique name, hairstyle, outfit, and price tag, strut around on the catwalk while bidders respond.

As Jemisin's essay emphasizes, the six-minute emotion picture flips the script on the genre's dominant whiteness by reversing the logic employed in *American Utopia*. Byrne's utopian collective incorporated tremendous diversity among a group that was at the same time united by their identical uniforms. But apart from one recurring shot of wholly identical figures vocalizing together, Monáe's android army largely consists of physically identical individuals atomized by their distinct outfits and the gendered and racialized types they thereby embody. Thus, where the former shows the power of intersectional anticapitalist collectives, "Many Moons" illustrates the ways in which racial capitalism's intertwined processes of racialized and gendered commodification strengthen its hold over us.

But "Many Moons" is much more than merely a critique of racial capitalism: it, too, offers its own pathway toward a utopian horizon. This transformative break is initiated just after the video's midpoint, when the focus shifts from Monáe's army of doppelgängers to Cindi Mayweather's on-stage presence. In a series of tight close-ups, her face is composited over black-and-white archive footage while she performs a "cybernetic chant"[31] that connects her Afrofuturist storyworld to racial capitalism's dystopian reality.

FIG. 19 "Many Moons—Official Short Film," emotion picture directed by Alan Ferguson. © 2008, Bad Boy Records/Wondaland.

The chant's long list of associative phrases once more underlines the obvious connection between the androids' less-than-human status and Black female flesh as a "limit case" for definitions of the human[32]: "Heroin user, coke head / Final chapter, death bed / Plastic sweat, metal skin / Metallic tears, mannequin." Over the course of this sequence, the footage behind her face becomes increasingly militaristic, with repeated shots of marching armies representing the destructive physical forces unleashed by racial capitalism. These powerful shots remind us that racism and state violence are deeply intertwined—and that we continue to live "in the eddies of their past and their *presence.*"[33] This militaristic montage finally culminates in an atomic bomb exploding in the footage, as a brief shot of Cindi shows her abruptly stripped down once more to her ghostly white endoskeleton.

Following this culmination of intersecting tensions, Cindi's performance is interrupted by a kind of malfunction: her eyes start blinking rapidly in close-up while her moves become increasingly frenzied and erratic. As the android breaks down, her body first levitates off the stage, until a beam of light erupts heavenward from her body before she slowly drifts back to the floor in a trancelike state. During this transformation, another identical android, identified as "Lady Maestra, Master of the Show Droids," approaches on horseback while mouthing the lyrics of the track's closing lullaby. A small army of androids in wedding dresses then encircles Cindi's prone body, their robotic eyes glowing from behind their veils, as Lady

Maestra voices lyrics of transformation, transcendence, and an escape to a better world:

> And when the world just treats you wrong
> Just come with us and we'll take you home
> Shan, Shan, Shan, Shan-gri La
> Na-na-na-naa, na-naa, naa-na-na-na-na

This ending, simultaneously painful and liberating, embraces a Black utopian tradition that draws its power from this central focus on escape from oppression.[34] Where Eurofuturist utopias have been grounded in colonialist energies,[35] Afrofuturist utopias open up horizons for escape from racial capitalism's powers of extraction, accumulation, and oppression.[36] Thus, as a close-up of Cindi shows her letting go and collapsing, an on-screen epitaph over a black screen spins a moment of defeat into one of utopian transformation: "I imagined the many moons in the sky lighting the way to freedom."

The "many moons" in this line do more than just clarify the meaning of the song's title, which isn't mentioned elsewhere in the lyric. It illuminates the dialectical organization of the utopian imagination, whose horizon of possibility only emerges in response to (and in dialogue with) forces of injustice and oppression.[37] This dialectic can be grounded in the performance of a transformative collective, as in *American Utopia*. Or, as in "Many Moons," it can take as its starting point a dystopian enhancement of racial capitalism's relentless practices of commodification, culminating in a moment of release as Mayweather allows herself to be "called home" to a utopian wonderland called Shangri-La.

But beyond explicitly articulating the emotion picture's message of hopeful transformation, the line expresses two essential aspects of the utopian imagination. First, it captures how utopia cannot be reduced to a blueprint that maps out the way to a predetermined outcome.[38] Utopia's radical potential lies precisely in its irreducible multiplicity—as a vector that opens up a multitude of possibilities for progress by unmooring reality from its "overwhelming taken-for-grantedness."[39] And second, the line emphasizes the productive power of imagination: the many moons that light the way toward a better, freer future only emerge by overcoming racial capitalism's stifling crisis of imagination, which paralyzes the development of meaningful political change.[40]

These liberatory anticapitalist ideas are fundamental to the Black utopian tradition. As we move through the latter-day stages of a capitalist system that has fallen into a chronic state of disrepair,[41] those rare moments in which the cracks of history open wide enough for actual change desperately need as big a variety of speculative scenarios for utopian futures.[42] "Our dystopian postdemocratic political moment requires imaginative thoughts. We need more rather than fewer utopian ideas about radical democracy and social freedom, more rather than fewer antiutopian critiques of American faith in free-market utopianism, religious fundamentalism, technological determinism, and racial progress. Black utopia can add to this chorus trying to generate them."[43] Once we recognize how capitalism was always already racialized, we also understand why the many moons of Black utopian thinking are the ones to guide us toward a postcapitalist horizon—not of futurity, but of true alterity.[44] Since the very concept of race was created as a mode of oppression, moving toward a future that will "expand the principles of fairness and opportunity to all members of society" is a process that should be driven and inspired by those Black voices with the most intimate knowledge of social inequality.[45] If we want to map out pathways to a better future, we therefore urgently require *new theory that is grounded in new history*.[46] Both these things are ultimately the product of a resolute Black radicalism that "advances as each generation assembles the data of its experience to an ideology of liberation."[47]

This ideology of liberation must therefore be constantly reinvented as our world's social and material organization is reshaped by residual and emergent forces. In this context, the twenty-first-century incarnation of racial capitalism has given rise to inspired critical and creative work by Black artists, writers, and theorists. Musician Boots Riley's film debut *Sorry to Bother You*, for which Monáe contributed to the soundtrack, has been one of the most provocative expressions of Black radicalism in contemporary cinema.

Sorry to Bother You: Racial Capitalism 2.0

Cassius "Cash" Green (played by Lakeith Stanfield) is all about the money: doubly named after the American "greenback" dollar, the protagonist of the 2018 movie *Sorry to Bother You* is stuck in a Sisyphean quest for financial stability. Living in contemporary Oakland, Cash inhabits a postindustrial landscape where neoliberalism's flexible accumulation has decimated labor unions,[48] and where employment options for the racialized and increasingly precarious working class are severely limited.[49] The choices available to Cash and his girlfriend Detroit (played by Tessa Thompson) are either working long hours for minimum wage at a sweatshop-like call center, or standing on street corners holding up signs pointing potential customers to increasingly rare storefront retailers.

But then, an opportunity unexpectedly materializes for the enterprising Cash. After experiencing how difficult it is for a Black call center employee to make a sale to white middle-class customers, a more experienced colleague (played by Danny Glover) lets him in on a secret, and explains to him why he should try using his "white voice":

"You wanna make some money here? Then read the script with a white voice."

"Well, people say I talk with a white voice anyway, so why it ain't helping me out?"

"Well, you don't talk white enough. I'm not talkin' about Will Smith white. That ain't white, that's just proper. I'm talking about the real deal."

"Okay, so like: 'Hello, Mr. Everet. Cassius Green here. *Sorry-to-bother-you . . .'*"

"No, no, you've got it all wrong. I'm not talking about sounding all nasal. It's, like, sounding like you don't have a care. You got your bills paid. You're happy about your future. You about ready to jump in your Ferrari out there after you get off this call. Put some real breath in there. Breezy, like: 'I don't really need this money.' You've never been fired—only laid off. It's not really a *white* voice. *It's what they wish they sounded like.* So, it's like what they think they're supposed to sound like."

This brief exchange perfectly captures the real meaning of whiteness within racial capitalism: how it means that "in order to succeed, you have to perform your personality in a way that is pleasing to white people."[50] This racist legacy derives from the establishment of a system of power in which citizenship was the exclusive domain of land-owning white men.[51] And even though the civil rights movement at least brought an end to the Jim Crow era and its legal enforcement of white supremacy, *Sorry to Bother You* cunningly dramatizes how racial capitalism in the digital era still limits wealth and privilege to those who manage to "enter the white race."[52] The film's central conceit of Black characters adopting an incongruously dubbed white voice[53] thereby brilliantly identifies race as a property relation above all else.

After gaining access to whiteness through his "puppet-master voodoo shit," Cash's swift ascent to the elevated rank of Power Caller transforms his life. But at the same time, his rising status puts him at odds with his friends and former colleagues, who are unionizing under the leadership of labor activist Squeeze (played by Steven Yeun). Initially dismissive of his friends' activism, Cash finally relents when he finds out that the Amazon-like corporation "WorryFree" has secretly been breeding a new species of indentured worker. The company's scientists have developed a proprietary gene-altering powder that transforms human beings into "Equisapiens" horsemen: a new form of dehumanized slave labor set to power the forms of postindustrial capitalism that the film satirizes.

Just as Monáe's "Many Moons" connects the fashion industry's gendered and racialized forms of commodification to the slave trade on which racial capitalism was built,[54] Riley's film powerfully evokes Malcolm X's crystal-clear statement that "you can't have capitalism without racism."[55] While our supposedly "postracial" present certainly allows for Black people to achieve individual wealth, the Equisapiens' telling combination of super- and sub-humanity marks them as the new generation of racialized slave labor, and therefore yet another continuation of racial capitalism's fundamentally racist forms of exploitation and accumulation.[56] And while Black folks—in this film as in real life—are dramatically overrepresented within this disposable workforce, the fact that anyone can be genetically "plasticized" simply underlines once more how race continues to operate as a technology that produces class relationships above all else.

As a satire, *Sorry to Bother You* insistently foregrounds the fact that the new digital economy simply operates as Racial Capitalism 2.0, perpetuating a white supremacist system of racialized exploitation. Writer-director Boots Riley comments explicitly on the racial organization of his high-tech dystopia in the audio commentary he recorded for the film, while at the same time expressing the joyful utopian energy that is produced dialectically from within this very system: "I wanted to talk about a life shaped by exploitation. About fighting for a say in our own lives. About how beauty, love, and laughter thrive and flourish under almost any circumstances. How capitalism basically started by stealing labor from Africans." Unlike the despair that typically dominates most Eurofuturist dystopias, *Sorry to Bother You* therefore focuses as much on the many moons of Black utopia as it does on critiquing racial capitalism. The film elegantly interweaves the Black radicalism of resurgent labor unions with Cash's dawning understanding of the intertwined relationship between racist oppression and capitalist exploitation, and, ultimately, an actual revolutionary movement in the Equisapiens' climactic rebellion.

While most of the main characters are men, this utopian energy is articulated most powerfully by the character played by frequent Janelle Monáe collaborator Tessa Thompson. In stark contract with Cash's repeated attempts to find a way into the system, Detroit is as uncaring about her own success as she is indifferent to his rising social status and growing material wealth. Instead, she subverts the existing social order in small and playful ways through her performance art, which extends from the fun she has in the creative twirling of signs in public space to an extended performance piece in an art gallery. In this sequence, Detroit appears on stage and invites the audience to bombard her with broken cell phones, used bullets, and blood—the literal waste produced by the global tech industry's exploitative practices. At the same time, Detroit contributes most of her spare time to organized movements that resist capitalist accumulation. Unlike Cash, her character's willingness to embrace beauty, love, and laughter repeatedly opens up utopian pathways that emerge from her creative abilities alongside her dedication to anticapitalist organizations.

This energy is extended on the movie's soundtrack album, on which Janelle Monáe collaborated with Riley's band The Coup for the track "Whathegirlmuthafuckinwannadoo." Vocalizing a single melody an octave apart, Riley and Monáe sing this rollicking up-tempo bop in perfect unison. The lyric offers a serenade to Detroit, thereby providing a sly continuation of the many ways in which Monáe has expressed her love for Tessa Thompson throughout her *Dirty Computer* project. The funky syncopations that make up the verses sing the praises of a Black woman whose creative instincts all run counter to racial capitalism's social order. Lines like "You know her, she won't let nobody control her" point to Detroit's independence from the male characters that surround her, while "Behind many great men is a woman with her dreams left on the ground" upends the sexist cliché about women providing emotional support for the men they serve. As Cash slowly realizes, Detroit is defined by her own goals and desires rather than her relationship with the male hero. Hence, the chorus's repeated lines: "Wanna keep her with you but the girl finna do / What the girl muthafuckin' wanna do."

To conclude this section, *Sorry to Bother You* gleefully embraces the anticapitalist politics of the Black radical tradition. Its slightly exaggerated depiction of racial capitalism in the digital age reveals the many ways in which the system isn't merely fundamentally antidemocratic,[57] but how political power remains wholly "organized around the central principle of race."[58] At the same time, this dystopian satire also reveals an underlying utopianism, which finds its source in the political organizing of labor unions and the joyful collectivism it engenders. The film thereby reproduces two key aspects of postcapitalist transformation that Jeremy Gilbert described in his recent book *Twenty-First Century Socialism*: "Any movement that wants to challenge the domination of capitalism and the legacy of neoliberalism must be equally ambitious and wide-ranging in its scope. It must seek to confront in every way the idea that humans are, or should be, inherently competitive, individualistic and asocial, while also refusing to have any truck with nationalist, racist, or misogynistic thinking. It must take this perspective into workplaces and political parties, but also into the domains of education, music, television, cinema, literature and philosophy."[59] In bringing these political energies together in a broadly accessible comedy film, *Sorry to Bother You* is a truly exciting expression of anticapitalist imagination. Outrageous inventions like the uncanny use of "white voice" and the human–horse hybrids communicate central truths about racial capitalism in the postindustrial era more effectively than any documentary film possibly could.

Above all else, Riley locates the seeds of this postcapitalist transformation in the creative performances of Black artists like Detroit, who consistently finds ways to subvert and undermine the system through pleasurable and creative performance. Detroit's role within the narrative thereby exemplifies the ways in which "Black utopias made aesthetics political."[60] By the same token, Janelle Monáe's contribution to the soundtrack album emphasizes how this kind of work has been derived from Black feminist creativity whose primary goal is a liberatory political transformation of racial capitalism's matrix of domination.[61] Not only does this in many ways typify Monáe's overall approach to media, performance, and creative production, but it also captures the dialectical nature of this transformative cultural work.

This returns us to yet another variation on the dialectic of oppression and resistance that has grounded Black feminist thought (as discussed in Vector 2). But where the intersections between gender, race, and sexuality define the groups that are most directly oppressed by racial capitalism's social hierarchy, anticapitalist resistance is grounded in a similarly dialectical form:

that of anger and love. Anticapitalist movements are fueled on the one hand by anger about the countless forms of systemic injustice that racial capitalism produces, and on the other by a love that is located in a deeply felt solidarity with those who suffer. This powerful dialectic opens up spaces that "produce a crack in the present, a disruption in the imposition of capitalist temporality" with the power to project a postcapitalist horizon.[62] In the following section of this final chapter, I therefore return once more to the expression of this dialectic in her own musical work.

"Stevie's Dream": Using Words of Love

Two separate short interludes interrupt the otherwise seamless flow of polished pop, funk, and neosoul on the *Dirty Computer* album: the first, "Jane's Dream," is a nineteen-second instrumental track that connects "Take a Byte" to "Screwed" through a simple repeated chord progression on guitar and synthesizer, written and played by composer and producer Jon Brion. This voiceless track provides a few bars of quiet introspection between two bright and boisterous tracks, giving musical shape to "terrifying nightmares about a near-future America full of abductions and secret detention centers—oddly like our own." The track's ominous pattern reflects this circular movement in its repeated guitar strums that first lead us upward, toward a hopeful, major-key alterity, only to retreat back downward, endlessly returning us to our minor-key present.

A similar circular pattern appears in the interlude's sister track "Stevie's Dream," which occurs between two songs near the album's end that express doubt, pain, and vulnerability: "Don't Judge Me" and "I'm So Afraid." But if the first dream may be read as a wordless expression of anxiety about an emergent dystopia, the second answers back in the voice of Monáe's mentor Stevie Wonder,[63] whose spoken words of reassurance she recorded at a dinner table:

Even when you're upset, use words of love
'Cause God is love, Allah is love, Jehovah is love
So, don't let your expressions, even of anger
Be confused or misconstrued
Turn them into words of expression
That can be understood by using words of love

Considering how the entire *Dirty Computer* project is structured around the concepts of reckoning, celebration, and reclamation, Wonder's words here fulfill an aspirational function that clarifies anticapitalism's dialectic of anger and love. While individual and collective anger over racial capitalism's systemic forms of oppression may seem obvious, the political necessity of love is too often and too easily overlooked. By incorporating Stevie Wonder's soothing words in the album's Reclamation section, Monáe emphatically turns the commodifiable ethic of self-love inside out. Instead, she subscribes to the idea that devotion to progressive political transformation firstly requires a truly radical love of the other.

Rather than a negation of anger, love is what ultimately directs our unwillingness to accept injustice. In order to move beyond racial capitalism, we must therefore first embrace what Paul Gilroy describes as a *politics of transfiguration*: a radically inclusive utopian horizon whose "basic desire is to conjure up and enact the new modes of friendship, happiness, and solidarity that are consequent on overcoming of the racial oppression on which modernity and its antinomy of rational, western progress as excessive barbarity relied."[64] Just as Black utopias have offered multiplying lines of flight from oppression, Gilroy's politics of transfiguration draws on a revolutionary ethic that is grounded in empathy, compassion, and love.

Croatian philosopher and anticapitalist organizer Srećko Horvat expressed this fundamental reciprocity between love and revolution most plainly in his book *The Radicality of Love*: "What is needed, in order to achieve a truly radical revolution, is love. . . . Love is communism for two. But love is as difficult as communism, and can often end up as tragic as communism. *Like revolution, true love is the creation of a new world*."[65] This statement of the radicality of love, which further expands Che Guevara's famous expression of its vital importance for truly revolutionary commitment,[66] can be readily identified throughout Janelle Monáe's work. The forbidden love between Cindi Mayweather and Anthony Greendown that starts a revolution, the nurturing love her character embodies in *Moonlight*'s journey toward queer Black self-acceptance, and the polyamorous eroticism that binds the three main characters in *Dirty Computer* are all expressions of the revolutionary power of love as the antidote to racial capitalism's dehumanizing logic.[67] In each case, it counters existing realities of oppression through transformative acts of imagination, in which intersectional Black feminism forms the conceptual anchor for this larger postcapitalist imagination.[68] And if solidarity is at the heart of truly feminist political practice, its politics of transfiguration yields visions of postcapitalist futures that are predicated not on clinical revolutionary fervor but on pleasure: a future that allows for crazy, classic lives of "more love," a world of "more good meals shared together in new and exciting ways."[69]

Such transformations present a tremendous challenge to the imagination. But this is precisely why utopian visions that illuminate horizons of possibility are so vital to anticapitalist movements. Across these horizons, new politics of transfiguration are shaped, molded, and energized by the songs, dances, performances, characters, stories, and desires of those who passionately resist.[70] So while it may appear easy to dismiss commercial pop culture as a frivolous exercise lacking substance or political potency, the creative and imaginative work done by performing artists is central, not secondary, to anticapitalism. For as Angela Davis learned from Cedric J. Robinson, the multiplicity of possibilities represented by political strategies aimed at true liberation can "only be evocatively represented in the realm of culture."[71]

In Monáe's own words, the primary imperative for an artist like herself is therefore "to bring awareness, your job is to be a rebel, your job is to start a revolution."[72] As a writer, producer, and performer whose work channels the political energy of the Black radical tradition, her work has the power to show us how fragile the current ordering of the world really is.[73] Not only is capitalism's power much more vulnerable than we tend to think, but it is also far less monolithic than we usually dare to imagine.[74] And this is precisely what makes Monáe's work such a potent expression of Black utopian postcapitalism: it shows stubbornly how even the grimmest capitalist dystopias are riddled with pockets of resistance with the power to spark a revolution.

These forms of resistance are powered by the radicality of love. Only by embracing the deep solidarity that emerges from the radicality of love can we move toward a politics of transfiguration, even if it exists in permanent tension with the anger we feel about the suffering brought about by racial capitalism's systemic injustice. This dialectic of anger and love is a primary site of struggle throughout Monáe's world-building, from the beginning of her *Metropolis* cycle through to her more recent albums, screen performances, and video productions. Therefore, as this chapter began with a discussion of her very first emotion picture "Many Moons," it will conclude with an analysis of her most recent track at the time of writing: "Turntables."

"What Is a Revolution without a Song?": Turning the Tables on Capitalism

As I was writing this book in the year 2020, the global COVID-19 pandemic threw the world into disarray. Sweeping across the globe during what would prove to be the last year of Donald Trump's disastrous presidency, the virus made racial capitalism's obscene disparities of wealth and privilege even more starkly visible. While billionaire CEOs of tech companies shamelessly lined their pockets, Black and brown communities across the globe were affected by the disease far more dramatically than affluent whites. And as liberals mindlessly parroted the words "We're all in this together," many soon learned that being stuck in the same storm doesn't necessarily mean that we're also in the same boat.

A key struggle in this tense and frightening year took place over voting rights in the U.S. elections. As one of racial capitalism's primary tools of oppression, Black voter disenfranchisement quickly became one of the key battlegrounds in a white supremacist president's hotly contested reelection. Besides appearing at protest marches and handing out free food through her #WondaLunch initiative,[75] Janelle Monáe responded to this struggle with a new emotion picture entitled "Turntables." The video accompanied a track she had written and produced together with her regular collaborator Nate "Rocket" Wonder for the documentary *All In: The Fight for Democracy* (2020). The film uses Stacey Abrams's gubernatorial campaign in Georgia to tell a larger story about the historical suppression of Black voting rights in American democracy. Abrams's narrow loss is both an inspiring tale of grassroots political organizing and a sobering reminder of how far there is still to go. Monáe's track closes the film as a powerful anthem that gives emotional energy to the filmmakers' explicit call to join the struggle and turn the tables on those who profit from racial capitalism.

The fundamental connection between music and politics typifies Monáe's impact as a socially engaged artist across all five of these vectors. It contributes to the essential project of social and political anticapitalist transformation. As Srećko Horvat has pointed out, "If we want to create a truly new political subjectivity, we need new songs. Metaphorically and literally."[76] And while a widely distributed documentary film may have the power to inform a large audience about the historical reality of racist voter suppression, a protest song like "Turntables" brings the subject to life

FIG. 20 "Turntables," emotion picture directed by Child. © 2020, Wondaland.

in more direct and visceral ways. This dynamic relationship between political transformation and creative production is at the very core of Monáe's output as an artist, performer, and activist. After all, as Monáe herself has asked: "What is a revolution without a song?"[77]

The Child-directed "Turntables" emotion picture brings together many of the key elements from across her career thus far. Set primarily within the Atlanta residence of a Black middle-class family, the video opens up an entry point into the past, present, and future of Black radicalism. It connects the family's everyday routine, at the breakfast table in present-day suburban Georgia, to the longer history of antiracist activism through the incorporation of a wide variety of archive footage. The video sutures these seemingly disparate elements together by a form of digital role-playing that vividly illustrates the importance of celebrity activism and media representation.

The emotion picture begins with images of Janelle Monáe walking along a beach, intercut with footage of a young Black girl wearing a VR headset before a large flatscreen television. The girl's hand gestures appear to control Monáe's movements as she pulls an LP out of her trench coat, opens up the suitcase she's carrying to reveal a portable turntable, and drops the needle on the record to start the track. While this introduction unfolds, we hear James Baldwin's voice reciting his famous refusal to give in to pessimism: "I can't be a pessimist because I am alive. To be a pessimist means that you have agreed that human life is an academic matter. So I am forced to be an optimist. I am forced to believe that we can survive whatever we must survive."[78] Baldwin's words poignantly complement Antonio Gramsci's famous phrase about the anticapitalist movement requiring pessimism of the intellect together with optimism of the will.[79] But Baldwin's deliberate wording also connects Gramsci's political energy to a more specific Black radicalism: one that relates these terms directly to the matter of survival in an anti-Black society.

As a prelude to the footage in the emotion picture and Monáe's own "Turntables" lyric, Baldwin's voice helps foreground what is at stake when it comes to voting rights: in a country where Black people are disproportionately arrested, incarcerated, and murdered by the state, democratic participation truly is a matter of life and death.[80] And while the documentary strongly urges Black citizens to join the struggle to exercise their voting rights, Monáe's song is a good deal more radical in its call to action. Not only does it call out specific problems regarding Black voter suppression in the United States, but the images and lyrics identify multiple systemic oppressions that are endemic to racial capitalism.

To reiterate a basic point on the relationship between capitalism and racism, the two are so deeply intertwined that they must be considered "intimately linked concepts."[81] As Black radicals from W.E.B. Du Bois and C.L.R. James to Angela Davis and Cedric J. Robinson have tirelessly pointed out, antiracism can therefore never be divorced from anticapitalism. It is precisely the conclusion Baldwin reached when he observed that the history of racism runs parallel to the history of capitalism, and that standing up to either one means attacking "the entire power structure of the western world."[82] In this sense, the system of racial capitalism represents the "burning house" in which Baldwin famously refused to be integrated.[83] In short, while his famous rejection of pessimism could clearly apply superficially to democratic participation, those words have far greater potency in their suggestion of a more radical postcapitalist future.

This utopianism is evident throughout the video, which prominently credits the singer as Janelle "Django Jane" Monáe. That credit explicitly connects this track to the Black radical persona she performed on *Dirty Computer* and its emotion picture (as discussed in Vector 3: Intersectionality). And while her wardrobe is different in "Turntables," her defiant posture, androgynous attire, rough-edged vocal performance, and syncopated rap-inflected delivery are very much the same. Through a finely tuned combination of montage and staging, the video underlines transhistorical vectors of racist oppression, antiracist protest, Black radicalism, and media representation: rapid cuts intertwine images of civil rights icons like Angela Davis and Muhammad Ali with contemporary voting rights campaigners like Stacey Abrams and footage from #BlackLivesMatter protests.

All the while, the suggestion remains that Monáe's character is an avatar the girl with the headset has chosen to control. Thus, by using her own Django Jane persona as the media extension of the young girl's VR-enhanced gaze, the video vividly unites past, present, and future into a single expression of Black radical transformation. At the same time, the middle-class domesticity of her household is intercut with images of fiery demonstrations. This effectively collapses the boundary between the public and the private sphere, while emphasizing that class mobility and respectability politics are no excuse for a potential retreat from the Black radical tradition.

Meanwhile, the lyric constitutes a full-throated expression of a revolutionary energy that is profoundly utopian. A line like "Got a new agenda with a new dream" can certainly be read as a liberal call to change the current regime and elect a new government. But a phrase like "new dream" resonates far more strongly with revolutionary aspirations than with a mere changing of the guard—especially if that political system remains grounded in racial capitalism's intersecting forms of oppression. This sentiment is further enhanced by the recurring line "America, you a lie / But the whole world 'bout to testify," followed shortly thereafter by the chorus, which is made up entirely of repeated variations of the phrase "And the tables 'bout to turn." This line cleverly combines different meanings of the word "revolution," as the visuals underline the idea that the physical revolutions of a record player can also strengthen and inspire social and political transformations. To borrow Cedric J. Robinson's memorable words, the song thereby mobilizes "culture as an organizing principle for revolutionary change."[84]

It is precisely this more radical meaning that Monáe has stressed in interviews and other media appearances. Talking to Zane Lowe on Apple Music, she emphasized this fundamental interconnection between music and politics:

We are changing things. The tables are turning. The rooster has come home to roost. So, this song is capturing direction. And when you think about a record, when you think about a record spinning, when you think about the revolutions per minute, it's all connected. And that is what this song means. This song doesn't mean that I'm the leader, that I'm here to tell you what to do, how to fix things. I'm simply watching, examining, and wanting to highlight all of the people who are on the front lines, fighting for our democracy, fighting against racial inequalities, fighting against white supremacy, fighting against systemic racism and systemic oppression.[85]

Her words here crystallize the shifting and porous line that exists between cultural production and political activism. While Janelle Monáe is frequently described as an activist, she has been careful—as she is here—not to claim a position of leadership, or even the label of "activist" without further qualification.[86] Her words rather amplify the idea that artists can shape their creative work to strengthen social and political movements. That there is a liberating potential to art and popular music. And that "the role of the artist is to make the revolution irresistible."[87] Songs like "Hell You Talmbout" and "Turntables" thereby help to breathe new life into existing movements by providing that "added dimension that political discourses sometimes fail to capture"[88]: a song to sing, a dance to share, and a struggle to join.

The "Turntables" emotion picture strengthens this political message through the prominent inclusion of trans, nonbinary, and other gender-nonconforming folk, who stand out among the individual video portraits that director Child intercuts with archive footage and images of protest marches. By contributing in this way to the important cultural work of flattening racial capitalism's hierarchies,[89] the video's revolutionary energy opens up a queer utopian horizon that is fundamentally anticapitalist: Monáe's performative worldmaking establishes an alternative view of the world that critiques "oppressive regimes of 'truth' that subjugate minoritarian people."[90] Thus, by bringing together racial capitalism's four main axes of oppression—race, gender, sexual identity, and class—in this ongoing performance, the postcapitalist utopia she projects is profoundly liberating in its radical queerness.

In this way, "Turntables" brings together the different vectors that run throughout her work as an artist, performer, and activist. It illustrates how her political world-building draws on Afrofuturism's chronopolitical dynamic by interweaving past and present to conjure up "an imaginary domain for radical democratic politics and life-forms outside of white supremacy, racial capitalism, and hetero-patriarchy."[91] It strengthens her critical focus on identifying and overturning the matrix of domination that is central to Black feminist thought. It demonstrates both her proud queerness and her networked collage of multiplying personas by fully embracing the relational organization of intersectionality. It offers a posthuman response to liberal humanism's profound negation of Black humanity. And its radical Black utopianism opens up a utopian postcapitalist horizon where a world of true freedom may yet prove to be possible if we sign our name on the dotted line.

Acknowledgments

Many people contributed to this book in different ways—far too many to list here. But the list of folks I want to thank must begin with Erik Steinskog, the eminent musicologist/philosopher/awesome dude who first introduced me to Janelle Monáe's music, and whose own written work on sonic Afrofuturism is exceptional. Similarly, my friend and confidant Gerry Canavan's unfailingly generous feedback and support have been invaluable form start to finish. And thirdly, my peerless coeditor and fellow curmudgeon Anindita Banerjee somehow always managed to dissuade me from abandoning this project at the most crucial moments.

For supporting and enabling my work on this project as it took more concrete form, I must thank the irrepressible and unbelievably prolific Frederick Aldama, who enthusiastically endorsed my take on this topic for his Global Media and Race book series. At Rutgers University Press, I want to thank executive editor Nicole Solano, whose helpful and communicative attitude helped keep everything on track throughout a long and tumultuous year. My sincere thanks as well to the anonymous peer reviewers, whose comments and suggestions regarding the proposal truly helped me avoid a number of traps and blind spots I had unwittingly set for myself. One reviewer's suggestions for further reading helped me see much more clearly what kind of book this might be—as well as clarifying for me what kind of approach was outside my grasp as a white man writing about race and gender.

During the writing process, several members of my extended online network gave me pointers, suggestions, and tips that were always warmly received. Some even offered to proofread one or more chapters and provided elaborate feedback. Endless thanks therefore to Jake Casella Brookins, Rachel Gillett, Barnita Bagchi, Geert Buelens, Ebissé Rouw, Kirti Advani, Jeroen Oomen, Francis Gene-Rowe, Walter Chaw, Jaap Kooijman, Pippa Sterk, Steve Shaviro, Nancy Jouwe, and my beloved father, Jim Forest.

I also want to express my thanks and admiration for Karen Palmer, the extraordinary filmmaker, artist, and public speaker who has come back from the future to tell us stories warning us about where we are headed. I had many wonderful discussions with Karen, and had hoped in the early stages to involve her as a collaborator in this project. Due in part to the ongoing pandemic, we were never able to make that work in practical terms. But I'm forever grateful for her input, her energy, and her support.

Two fellows deserve special mention for selflessly proofreading truly substantial chunks of this work-in-progress as it developed. Harry Warwick combined his unfailing eye for dangling participles and mixed metaphors with an acute sense of theory, logic, and structure. His detailed feedback strengthened the text immeasurably, while also pushing me to recognize and revise many of the weaknesses in my application of theoretical concepts. My dear friend Mark Bould not only provided similarly detailed editorial feedback on early drafts of the chapters, but also shared with me the manuscript of the book he was writing around the same time. I'm as grateful to his generosity as I am envious of his abilities as a writer. As Dominic Toretto would say, "You'll always be with me, and you'll always be my brother."

I also want to thank my colleagues and students at Utrecht University. Working on this book had a powerful impact on the way I perceived my obligations as a teacher, a scholar, and a human being. The enthusiastic responses I received from my own academic community, as I increasingly focused my research and teaching on race and racism, were a great source of confidence and inspiration. And the online screenings I organized of Janelle Monáe's *Dirty Computer* were among the most memorable teaching experiences I've ever had.

Writing and researching this book during all the disruptions of the COVID-19 pandemic in 2020 and early 2021 inevitably increased the overall pressure on my home life and family. Above all else, I really want to thank my partner and kids for remaining as understanding as anyone could reasonably be under these circumstances. My love and gratitude extend as well to my parents and siblings. Both my parents have been lifelong activists, and the many conversations I've had with them about the book's subject matter and their own experience with social movements and musical activism have been tremendously valuable, as has their unfailing love and warm encouragement.

Finally, my deepest gratitude and respect for the person of Janelle Monáe herself. Given my own lived experience as a cis white man, I can only imagine how meaningful her music, performances, and activism must be to all the "dirty computers" who endure oppression and injustice for being who they are. But as a writer, performer, and activist who always speaks up for the marginalized, her voice and vision have been a constant source of inspiration to me, as I'm sure they will continue to be for countless others.

For me, this was a book that I had to write. As doubtful as I remained throughout as to whether I was the right person to write this book, I nevertheless felt absolutely compelled to continue. A truly magnetic artist, Janelle Monáe has not only inspired me—her work has set me on a path that has fundamentally altered my perception of the world. Listening to her music, watching her screen performances, witnessing her stage acts, listening to her words, and researching her influences opened the door to new ways of thinking and writing—as I hope it will for those who read this book. Peace.

Notes

Introduction

1 Throughout the book, I capitalize the word Black and its variants, as suggested by Rachele Kanigel in *The Diversity Style Guide* (London: Wiley-Blackwell, 2019).

2 Janelle Monáe, *Metropolis: The Chase Suite—Special Edition*, Bad Boy Records/Wondaland 7567-89932-8, 2008, compact disc.

3 Monáe's first major-label release was preceded by an independently produced collection of tracks entitled *The Audition*, one of which ("Cindi") laid the groundwork for her subsequent Afrofuturist world-building. This self-financed demo album was distributed by Monáe herself, who sold copies from the trunk of her car, with fewer than 500 physical copies believed to be in existence.

4 Janelle Monáe, *The ArchAndroid*, Bad Boy Records/Wondaland 7567-89898-3, 2010, compact disc.

5 From the start of her musical career, Monáe has referred to her video productions as "emotion pictures" rather than music videos. I use the term throughout the book to acknowledge and respect this terminological preference, except for occasional cases where its use creates inelegant repetition.

6 Janelle Monáe, *The Electric Lady*, Bad Boy Records/Wondaland 536210-2, 2013, compact disc.

7 Janelle Monáe, *Dirty Computer*, Bad Boy Records 7567-86579-3, 2018, compact disc.

8 *Electric Dreams*, episode 2, "Autofac," directed by Peter Horton, written by Travis Beacham and Philip K. Dick, featuring Janelle Monáe, Juno Temple, and David Lyons, aired January 12, 2018, on Amazon Prime, https://www.amazon.com/Philip-K-Dicks-Electric-Dreams/dp/B075NTXMN9.

9 Jenkins, *Convergence Culture*, 97–98.

10 Neil Archer, *Twenty-First Century Hollywood*, 41–42.

11 Jenkins, *Convergence Culture*, 97–98.

12 OED definition.

13 Gilles Deleuze defines a vector field as the "*complete determination of a problem* given in terms of the existence, number and distribution of points that are its condition." See Deleuze, *Time and Repetition*, 177.

14 For an elaborate discussion of Whitehead's relevance to contemporary theories of speculative realism, see Shaviro, *The Universe of Things*.

15 McKittrick, *Dear Science*, 51–52.

16 McKittrick, *Dear Science*, 5.

17 Brock, *Distributed Blackness*, 218.

18 Robinson, *Black Marxism*.

19 Thomas, *The Dark Fantastic*, 169.

20 Collins, *Black Feminist Thought*, 15–16.

21 Collins, 246–250.

22 Crenshaw, "Mapping the Margins," 1241–1299.

23 Collins, *Intersectionality*, 7–8.

24 Fanon, *Black Skin, White Masks*, 2.

25 Atanasoski and Vora, *Surrogate Humanity*, 5.

26 Jackson, *Becoming Human*, 18–19.

27 Olufemi, *Feminism, Interrupted*.

28 Books like Morgan's *She Begat This* and Abdurraqib's *Go Ahead in the Rain* are magnificent examples of such personally engaged studies that have yet to be written about Janelle Monáe.

Chapter 1   Vector 1: Afrofuturism

1 Womack, *Afrofuturism*, 16.

2 Carrington, *Speculative Blackness*, 13.

3 Dery, "Black to the Future," 180.

4 Dyer, *White*, 36.

5 Lavender, *Afrofuturism Rising*, 196.

6 McKittrick, *Dear Science*, 60.

7 Gilroy, *The Black Atlantic*.

8 Robinson, *Black Marxism*, 2.

9 Robinson's theoretical work builds on the groundbreaking scholarship of pioneering Black Marxists like W.E.B. Du Bois and C.L.R. James.

10 Robinson, *Black Marxism*, 4.

11 Jackson, *Becoming Human*, 18.

12 David Roediger has proposed the term "white advantage" as an alternative to "white privilege," as it makes it easier for poor white people to understand that it entails not so much automatic rewards but the absence of barriers. See Roediger, *Class, Race, and Marxism*, 20–21.

13 Carrington, *Speculative Blackness*, 16–17.

14 A Google search for what I thought was a neologism of my own depressingly yielded a few blog entries on white supremacist websites and forums calling for a renewed dedication to "Eurofuturism" as a racist response to Afrofuturism's growing visibility. It falls within the same reactionary category as more commonly used racist phrases like "white genocide," "forced diversity," and "The Great Replacement."

15 Jackson, *Becoming Human*, 4.

16 Zamalin, *Black Utopia*, 11.

17 Colson Whitehead's Afrofuturist zombie novel *Zone One* brilliantly uses the assumption of whiteness as a "neutral" identity, only to confront the reader with their own racial bias by revealing in the final twist that the generic and racially unspecified first-person narrator is Black.

18 Rieder, *Colonialism and the Emergence of Science Fiction*, 30.

19 Thomas, *The Dark Fantastic*, 9–10.

20 Thomas, 159.

21 Jenkins, Peters-Lazaro, and Shresthova, *Popular Culture and the Civic Imagination*, 5

22 Robinson, *Cedric J. Robinson: On Racial Capitalism*, 22.

23 Lavender, *Afrofuturism Rising*, 2.

24 The prolific Nigerian American author Nnedi Okorafor has rejected Afrofuturism in favor of the term "Africanfuturism." This alternate term distinguishes a subgenre that is "specifically and more directly rooted in African culture, history, mythology, and point-of-view as it then branches into the Black Diaspora, and [that] does not privilege or center the West." See Okorafor's website for more information: http://nnedi.blogspot.com/2019/10/africanfuturism-defined.html.

25 Carrington, *Speculative Blackness*, 22–23.

26 While *Metropolis: The Chase Suite* is Monáe's first major-label release as well as her paradigmatic premiere concept album, the basic premise had previously been sketched out in the tracks "Metropolis" and "Cindi" on her self-financed and privately distributed demo album *The Audition* (2003). This demo album has never had an official release, but it can be easily downloaded.

27 Brooks, *Liner Notes for the Revolution*, 115.

28 This framework is explored more fully in Vector 2: Black Feminism.

29 Her use of the heteronormative "star-crossed lovers" trope also reinforces the gender binary in ways that undermine her storyworld's queer utopia—see Vector 3: Intersectionality for a more detailed discussion of this topic.

30 Abdurraqib, *A Little Devil in America*, "I Would Like to Give Merry Clayton Her Roses."

31 "Janelle Monáe: 'Many Moons' Official Short Film (HD)," YouTube video, 6:38, posted by Janelle Monáe, April 5, 2009, https://www.youtube.com/watch?v=EZyyORSHbaE.

32 For a more elaborate analysis of the "Many Moons" emotion picture, see Vector 5: Postcapitalism.

33 The orchestra is identified in the credits as The Wondaland String Ensemble together with The Wondaland Woodwinds.

34 Lordi, *The Meaning of Soul*, 9.

35 Tolkien, "On Fairy-Stories," 138–141.

36 See Wolf, *Building Imaginary Worlds*, 24–27.

37 Wekker, *White Innocence*.

38 Thomas, *The Dark Fantastic*, 28.

39 Verghese, "Absent Center."

40 Eshun, "Further Considerations on Afrofuturism," 297.

41 Brown, *Black Utopias*, 17.

42 Yusoff, *A Billion Black Anthropocenes or None*, 26–27.

43 Rieder, *Colonialism and the Emergence of Science Fiction*, 30.

44 Berardi, *After the Future*, 25.

45 Rieder, *Colonialism and the Emergence of Science Fiction*, 5.
46 Crary, *24/7*.
47 Bould, "The Ships Landed Long Ago," 177–186.
48 Zamalin, *Black Utopia*, 16.
49 Du Bois, *The Souls of Black Folk*, 8.
50 Mbembe, *Necropolitics*, 173.
51 Yusoff, *A Billion Black Anthropocenes or None*, 69.
52 Fanon, *Black Skin, White Masks*, 117.
53 Ahmed, "A Phenomenology of Whiteness," 157.
54 Singh, *Race and America's Long War*, 50.
55 Butler, *Kindred*.
56 Canavan, *Octavia E. Butler*, 61.
57 Ignatiev, "Without a Science of Navigation," 290.
58 Whitehead, *The Underground Railroad*.
59 "Antebellum (2020 Movie) Official Teaser—Janelle Monáe," YouTube video, 0:59, posted by Lionsgate Movies, November 21, 2019, https://www.youtube.com/watch?v=mXcZ7WDsVwk.
60 Mbembe, *Necropolitics*, 59–60.
61 See Vector 4: Posthumanism for an extended discussion of the relationship between Blackness and the figure of the doppelgänger.
62 Sharpe, *In the Wake*, 15.
63 Hartman, *Scenes of Subjection*, 3.
64 Daniels, "Antebellum is 2020's Worst Movie."
65 Davis, "How Black Women Are Reshaping Afrofuturism."
66 Collins, "'Antebellum' is a Revenge Fantasy."
67 Weheliye, *Habeas Viscus*, 90.
68 For a book-length study of sonic Afrofuturism, see Steinskog, *Afrofuturism and Black Sound Studies*.
69 Zuberi, "The Transmolecularization of [Black] Folk," 991–996.
70 Royster, *Sounding Like a No-No*, 88–115.
71 Bird, "Climbing Aboard the Mothership," 29–33.
72 In a historic acknowledgment of the P-Funk collective's cultural importance, a replica of the band's massive Mothership stage prop was inducted into the Smithsonian National Museum of African American History and Culture in 2011.
73 Kreiss, "Performing the Past to Claim the Future," 200.
74 Womack, *Afrofuturism*, 80.
75 Aceves, "We Travel the Spaceways."
76 Steinskog, *Afrofuturism and Black Sound Studies*, 180–187.
77 Royster, *Sounding Like a No-No*, 60–87.
78 Kennedy, "Commentary: On Its 40th Anniversary"; Hassler-Forest, "Utopian Afrofuturism in *The Wiz*," 88–90.
79 Werner, *A Change Is Gonna Come*, 245–246.
80 "Billy Ocean—Loverboy (Official HD Video)," YouTube video, 4:48, posted by Billy Ocean, September 20, 2019, https://www.youtube.com/watch?v=tyrowWnlNnQ.
81 "2Pac—California Love feat. Dr. Dre (Dirty) (Music Video) HD," YouTube video, 5:28, posted by Seven Hip-Hop, May 30, 2020, https://www.youtube.com/watch?v=mwgZalAFNhM.

82 "Janet Jackson—Rhythm Nation (Official Music Video)," YouTube video, 4:26, posted by Janet Jackson, June 17, 2009, https://www.youtube.com/watch?v =OAwaNWGLMoc.

83 Steinskog, "Michael Jackson and Afrofuturism," 126–140.

84 "Michael Jackson—Remember The Time (Official Video)," YouTube video, 9:16, posted by Michael Jackson, October 3, 2009, https://www.youtube.com/watch?v =LeiFFogvqcc.

85 "Michael Jackson, Janet Jackson—Scream (Official Video)," YouTube video, 4:47, posted by Michael Jackson, October 3, 2009, https://www.youtube.com/watch?v =oP4A1K4lXDo.

86 Rieder, *Science Fiction and the Mass Cultural Genre System*, 140.

87 English and Kim, "Now We Want Our Funk Cut," 218.

88 Valnes, "Janelle Monáe and Afro-Sonic Feminist Funk."

89 Jones, "'Tryna Free Kansas City,'" 43.

90 Meikle, *Adaptations in the Franchise Era*, 8–9.

91 "Michael Jackson—Thriller (Official Video)," YouTube video, 13:42, posted by Michael Jackson, October 3, 2009, https://www.youtube.com/watch?v =sOnqjkJTMaA.

92 Wright, "The Boy Kept Swinging," 68.

93 Vernallis, *Experiencing Music Video*, x.

94 Kooijman, "The Boxed Aesthetic," 236.

95 Railton and Watson, *Music Video and the Politics of Representation*, 58.

96 Occasional exceptions in which a pop star plays a character without simultaneously performing their own star persona, like Kate Bush's "Cloudbusting" music video, merely serve to underline the ubiquity of this general convention.

97 Bowrey, "The New Intellectual Property," 196.

98 Donnelly, *Justify My Love*, "Part 2."

99 Railton and Watson, *Music Video and the Politics of Representation*, 37.

100 Gilroy, *The Black Atlantic*, 102.

101 Royster, *Sounding Like a No-No*, 28.

102 Canavan, "The Limits of *Black Panther*'s Afrofuturism."

103 Ringen, "How Singer-Songwriter, Actress-Activist Janelle Monáe Gets So Much Done."

104 Hassler-Forest, "Vision Quest or Fool's Gold," 236.

105 In the sketch, Pryor uses the n-word here—which he stopped using in his comedy shortly thereafter, and which I prefer not to reproduce unless it is part of a quotation in which it performs a meaningful function.

106 Pryor, "Black Hollywood," *Bicentennial Nigger*, © 1976, Warner Brothers Records, 8122-79642-9C, Compact Disc.

107 A painfully apropos illustration here is the robot character Box in *Logan's Run*, who was voiced by Black actor Roscoe Lee Brown. Adding insult to injury, the movie not only presents an all-white future, but it continues to incorporate invisible Black labor in the role of a mechanical slave. See Nama, *Black Space*, 24–27.

108 Brown, *Black Utopias*, 8.

109 Zamalin, *Black Utopia*, 14.

110 Brown, *Black Utopias*, 15.

111 Gilroy, *The Black Atlantic*, 71.

112 Terry Eagleton, *Hope without Optimism.*
113 Bonneuil and Fressoz, *The Shock of the Anthropocene.*
114 Augé, *The Future,* 3.
115 Monbiot, *Out of the Wreckage,* 6.
116 Neiwert, *Alt-America*; Mondon and Winter, *Reactionary Democracy.*
117 Zamalin, *Black Utopia,* 10.
118 See Vector 3: Intersectionality for a more detailed discussion of the *Dirty Computer* album.
119 At the time of writing, a further transmedia expansion of the *Dirty Computer* project was announced: Janelle Monáe's literary debut *The Memory Librarian and Other Stories from the World of Dirty Computer* was announced for publication in 2022.
120 At the same time, it has the practical advantage of facilitating the use of the individual segments as more traditional stand-alone music videos that help promote Monáe's music.
121 The sight of two Black women rescuing a weakened Black man from captivity subtly strengthens the emotion picture's Black feminist agenda.
122 Bloch, *The Principle of Hope.*
123 Muñoz, *Cruising Utopia,* 99.
124 Muñoz, 91.
125 Zamalin, *Black Utopia,* 142.
126 See Vector 3: Intersectionality for a more detailed discussion of *Dirty Computer.*
127 Yusoff, *A Billion Black Anthropocenes or None,* xii.

Chapter 2   Vector 2: Black Feminism

1 Collins, *Black Feminist Thought,* 8.
2 The phrase is commonly attributed to American civil rights activist Marian Wright Edelman.
3 Yuen, *Reel Inequality,* 2.
4 Erigha, *The Hollywood Jim Crow,* 4–5.
5 Shetterly, *Hidden Figures.*
6 In 2020, the agency's Washington headquarters was renamed the Mary W. Jackson NASA Headquarters, due at least in part to the film's tremendous success.
7 Monáe had previously done voice acting for the film *Rio 2* (2014) and had appeared in *Moonlight* (2016), an independent film that was released just two months before *Hidden Figures,* but which was limited in its initial theatrical run to metropolitan arthouse theaters.
8 *Hidden Figures* yielded a worldwide gross of $236 million against an estimated production budget of $25 million.
9 Among the many public and private initiatives inspired by the film was a U.S. State Department–organized, publicly funded exchange program for women. See White, "Hidden Figures."
10 Gilbert, *Anticapitalism and Culture.*
11 "The ethics of Western society informed by imperialism and capitalism are personal rather than social. They teach us that the individual good is more important than the collective good, and consequently that individual change is of greater significance than collective change." hooks, *Feminist Theory,* 30.
12 Jones, "Janelle Monáe's Radical Rebellion."

13 See Marable, *Beyond Black and White*.

14 Smith, "Altered States," 34–56.

15 Gray, *Show Sold Separately*, 5.

16 Smith, "Intersectional Feminism Triumphs in 'Hidden Figures'."

17 hooks, *Feminist Theory*, 53.

18 Lorde, *Sister Outsider*, 51.

19 hooks, *Feminist Theory*, 53.

20 Nash, *Black Feminism Reimagined*, 5.

21 Donnelly, *Justify My Love*, "Part 3."

22 Aghoro, "Agency in the Afrofuturist Ontologies," 330.

23 Delphy, *Separate and Dominate*.

24 Delphy, 25.

25 Delphy, 15.

26 Dyer, *White*, 3.

27 Yuen, *Reel Inequality*, 56–57.

28 Verghese, "Absent Center."

29 Dyer, *White*, 9.

30 Collins, *Black Feminist Thought*, 246.

31 Taylor, ed., *How We Get Free*.

32 Nash, *Black Feminism Reimagined*, 7.

33 hooks, *Feminist Theory*, 16.

34 Gilroy, *The Black Atlantic*, 87.

35 Gilroy, 87.

36 Lordi, "Human After All."

37 Arruzza, Bhattacharya, and Fraser, *Feminism for the 99%*.

38 Morales, "Exclusive: Janelle Monáe Talks."

39 Johnston, "Kesha and Dr. Luke."

40 Fisher, "Janelle Monáe Delivered."

41 Marable, *Beyond Black and White*, "History and Black Consciousness: The Political Culture of Black America."

42 Marable, *Beyond Black and White*, "History and Black Consciousness: The Political Culture of Black America."

43 Marable, *Beyond Black and White*, "Beyond Racial Identity Politics: Toward a Liberation Theory for Multicultural Democracy."

44 Fraser, *Fortunes of Feminism*, 162.

45 Fraser, 162.

46 Fraser, 171.

47 Marable, *Beyond Black and White*, "History and Black Consciousness: The Political Culture of Black America."

48 Thomas, *The Dark Fantastic*, 159–164.

49 Collins, *Black Feminist Thought*, 247–250.

50 English and Kim, "Now We Want Our Funk Cut," 222.

51 Jones, "Tryna Free Kansas City," 43.

52 Himes, "Janelle Monáe: Imagining Her Own Future."

53 See Vector 4: Posthumanism for a more detailed analysis of definitions of "the human" regarding race and gender.

54 The lyric of her song "Sincerely, Jane," which first appeared on *Metropolis: The Chase Suite*, emphasizes the historical connection between the objectification and

sexualization of young Black women's bodies by the culture industry: "Danger, there's danger / When you take your clothes off / All your dreams go down the drain, girl."

55 Lester, "Janelle Monáe: 'It's True. I Am Part-Android.'"

56 Long cultural histories of male drag performance and blackface traditions vividly attest to this asymmetrical organization of representational performance. For the latter, see Robinson, *Forgeries of Memory & Meaning*, 127–179.

57 Collins, *Black Feminist Thought*, 15.

58 Collins, 292.

59 Collins, 219.

60 Collins, 219.

61 See Vector 1: Afrofuturism for a more detailed discussion of this album's narrative sequencing.

62 For an in-depth study of *The ArchAndroid*, see Favreau, *The ArchAndroid (33 1/3)*.

63 Gilbert and Pearson, *Discographies*, 31–33.

64 Taylor, *How We Get Free*, "Introduction."

65 Wallace, *Black Macho*.

66 See Vector 4: Posthumanism for a discussion of Monáe's multiple negotiations of the human.

67 The fourth track on *The ArchAndroid*, and one that makes up part of a gapless "mini-symphony" with the two preceding tracks.

68 English and Kim, "Now We Want Our Funk Cut," 224.

69 Janelle Monáe, "Janelle Monáe—Tightrope [feat. Big Boi] (Video)," YouTube video, 5:12, posted by "Janelle Monáe," April 1, 2010, https://www.youtube.com/watch?v=pwnefUaKCbc.

70 Breihan, "Best New Track: Janelle Monáe, 'Tightrope' (ft. Big Boi)."

71 Director Wendy Morgan, quoted in Favreau, "1. Tightrope."

72 McKittrick, *Dear Science and Other Stories*, 161.

73 Brooks, *Liner Notes for the Revolution*, 115.

74 Brooks, 116.

75 Janelle Monáe, "Janelle Monáe—Cold War [Official Music Video]," YouTube video, 3:43, posted by "Janelle Monáe," August 5, 2010, https://www.youtube.com/watch?v=lqmORiHNtN4.

76 For a more detailed analysis of this music video in an earlier book, see Hassler-Forest, *Science Fiction, Fantasy, and Politics*, 185–190.

77 Collins, *Black Feminist Thought*, 142–145.

78 Vernallis, *Unruly Media*, 34–35.

79 Shaviro, *Digital Music Videos*, 74.

80 Benjamin, *Race after Technology*, 160.

81 Benjamin, 110–111.

82 Redmond, "This Safer Space," 398.

83 Benjamin, *Race after Technology*, 80.

84 Lordi, "'Calling All Stars.'"

85 The character is performed by album coproducer and longtime Monáe collaborator Chuck Lightning.

86 Lordi, "Black Radio," 45.

87 Bascomb, "Freakifying History," 60.

88 The terms are quoted from the liner notes as listed in the CD booklet.

89 "Janelle Monáe—Q.U.E.E.N. feat. Erykah Badu [Official Video]," YouTube video, 6:04, posted by "Janelle Monáe," May 2, 2013, https://www.youtube.com /watch?v=tEddixS-UoU.

90 Murchison, "Let's Flip It!," 88–89.

91 Roediger, *How Race Survived U.S. History*, 157.

92 Benjamin, *Race after Technology*, 195.

93 Rieder, *Colonialism and the Emergence of Science Fiction*, 110.

94 Aghoro, "Agency in the Afrofuturist Ontologies," 332.

95 Rieder, *Colonialism and the Emergence of Science Fiction*, 7.

96 Flies have a long history as metaphorical embodiments of breakdown in hierarchical organizations of power in politics, science, and other forms of white cis-het patriarchy. See, for instance, *Brazil* (1985), *The Fly* (1986), *The Game* (1997), *Breaking Bad* episode "Fly" (2010) and the first episode of science fiction series *Westworld* (2016).

97 Janelle Monáe, quoted in Redmond and Phillips, "The People Who Keep on Going," 220.

98 Russell, *Glitch Feminism*, "Introduction."

99 See, for instance, the track "Come Alive (War of the Roses)" on *The ArchAndroid*: "When everything is wrong, just dance inside your mind/And you'll come alive."

100 Bascomb, "Freakifying History," 65.

101 The song's title had originally been conceived as "Q.U.E.E.R."; see Spanos, "Janelle Monáe Frees Herself."

102 Benjamin, "Janelle Monáe says 'Q.U.E.E.N.' Is for the 'Ostracized & Marginalized.'"

103 Benjamin, *Race after Technology*, 44–45.

104 Atanasoski and Vora, *Surrogate Humanity*, 13.

105 Russell, *Glitch Feminism*, "Introduction."

106 Kreiss, "Performing the Past to Claim the Future," 200.

107 Amin, "The Booty Don't Lie," 248.

108 Collins, *Black Feminist Thought*, 157.

109 Collins, 182.

110 The line also references the hugely influential science fiction author Philip K. Dick, whose novel *Do Androids Dream of Electric Sheep?* was adapted into the film *Blade Runner*.

111 Monáe would return to this role on *Dirty Computer* with the track "Django Jane," which is discussed in more detail in Vector 3: Intersectionality.

112 David, "Afrofuturism and Post-Soul Possibility," 698.

Chapter 3   Vector 3: Intersectionality

1 Haile, "Janelle Monáe, *Dirty Computer*."

2 Spanos, "Janelle Monáe Frees Herself."

3 Olufemi, *Feminism, Interrupted*, ch. 4.

4 Monro, *Gender Politics*, ch. 2.

5 Olufemi, *Feminism, Interrupted*, ch. 10.

6 "APES**T—THE CARTERS," posted by "Beyoncé," June 16, 2018, 6:04, YouTube video, https://www.youtube.com/watch?v=kbMqWXnpXcA.

7 Allen, "Why Organizers Are Fighting."

8 Hassler-Forest, "'The Lion King' Is a Fascistic Story."
9 Irakoze, "Why We Must Be Careful."
10 Davis, *Women, Race & Class.*
11 Collins, *Intersectionality as Critical Social Theory,* 7–8.
12 Nash, *Black Feminism Reimagined,* 9.
13 Nash, 24.
14 Collins, *Intersectionality as Critical Social Theory,* 44–50.
15 It is important to note here that the distinction between Black feminism and intersectionality is often more one of the meanings and associations activated by the terms themselves rather than a fundamental difference in their theoretical or practical agendas: many of the foundational voices in Black feminism certainly foregrounded queerness and sexual identity alongside race, gender, and class, and the Combahee River Collective Statement was obviously intersectional far before that term was coined. But where the term "Black feminism" has served to maintain a primary focus on race, gender, and class, the introduction of the word "intersectionality" has encouraged more complex, inclusive, and multidirectional organization of social power and identity politics.
16 While the increasingly ubiquitous presence of intersectionality as a method, theory, and praxis has enhanced the reach of concerns that have been central to Black feminist thought, its more inclusive framework has also been used to shift attention away from marginalized groups.
17 Collins, *Intersectionality as Critical Social Theory,* 29–30.
18 Nash, *Black Feminism Reimagined,* 70.
19 Ferguson, *One-Dimensional Queer,* 21.
20 Dijck, *The Culture of Connectivity,* 21.
21 Gainous and Wagner, *Tweeting to Power,* 8.
22 Bleznak, "Why Janelle Monáe says 1 'I May Destroy You.'"
23 Collins, *Intersectionality as Critical Social Theory,* 63–64.
24 Collins, 220–221.
25 Jung, "How Michaela Coel Wrote *I May Destroy You*'s Dreamlike Ending."
26 I am reminded of these words from bell hooks (*Feminist Theory,* 36): "Suggesting a hierarchy of oppression exists, with sexism in first place, evokes a sense of competing concerns that is unnecessary."
27 Collins, *Intersectionality as Critical Social Theory,* 47.
28 Collins, 63.
29 Collins, 44.
30 Nash, *Black Feminism Reimagined,* 24.
31 Monro, *Gender Politics,* ch. 2.
32 Collins, *Intersectionality as Critical Social Theory,* 50.
33 For a more complete discussion of *Dirty Computer,* see Dan Hassler-Forest, *Janelle Monáe's* Dirty Computer.
34 Leight, "Janelle Monae Talks Enlisting Brian Wilson."
35 Mieli, *Towards a Gay Communism,* ch. 1.
36 Setaro, "Reckoning, Celebration, and Reclamation."
37 See Vector 5: Postcapitalism for a more detailed discussion of "Stevie's Dream."
38 Wortham, "How Janelle Monáe Found Her Voice."
39 Nash, *Black Feminism Reimagined,* 70.

40 The words are read out by Pastor Dr. Sean McMillan, whose powerful diction and deep vocal timbre evokes Dr. Martin Luther King Jr., both in content and in form.
41 Muñoz, *Cruising Utopia*, 40.
42 Muñoz, 32.
43 Muñoz, 30.
44 See Vector 1: Afrofuturism for a description of the emotion picture's narrative structure.
45 See the final section of Vector 1: Afrofuturism for a more detailed description of the *Dirty Computer* emotion picture.
46 Bryant, "Janelle Monáe is 'Young, Black, Wild, and Free.'"
47 Muñoz, *Cruising Utopia*, 25.
48 Brooks, *Liner Notes for the Revolution*, 119.
49 Collins, *Intersectionality as Critical Social Theory*, 50.
50 Geffen, "Janelle Monáe Steps into Her Bisexual Lighting."
51 Muñoz, *Cruising Utopia*, 32.
52 Penney, *After Queer Theory*, ch. 1.
53 While Oscar Wilde's writing includes a few similar-sounding phrases, the attribution of this line is most likely apocryphal.
54 This distinction vividly illustrates the deep linkages that exist between homophobia and misogyny.
55 In the song's music video, Monáe is seen in a few shots wearing a shirt bearing the words "Subject Not Object."
56 A delightful part of the *Dirty Computer* stage show was the moment where Monáe's four dancers would pull out brightly colored super-soaker water pistols and douse the overheated audience in their cooling spray.
57 "Janelle Monáe—Django Jane [Official Music Video]," YouTube video, 3:16, posted by "Janelle Monáe," February 22, 2018, https://www.youtube.com/watch?v=mTjQq5rMlEY.
58 Brown, "New Formation."
59 Yates-Richard, "'Hell You Talmbout,'" 46.
60 Monáe, "Django Jane: What Inspired This song?"
61 Mulvey, "Visual Pleasure and Narrative Cinema," 6–18.
62 Cuboniks, *The Xenofeminist Manifesto*, 33.
63 Zamalin, *Black Utopia*, 15.
64 Muñoz, *Cruising Utopia*, 56.
65 Janelle Monáe, "Janelle Monáe—PYNK [Official Music Video]," YouTube video, 4:28, posted by "Janelle Monáe," April 10, 2018, https://www.youtube.com/watch?v=PaYvlVR_BEc.
66 Penney, *After Queer Theory*, ch. 1.
67 Chu, *Females*, ch. 2.
68 Gilroy, *The Black Atlantic*, 43.
69 Olufemi, *Feminism, Interrupted*, ch. 4.
70 Steinmetz, "The Transgender Tipping Point."
71 Olufemi, *Feminism, Interrupted*, ch. 4.
72 Monro, *Gender Politics*, ch. 5.
73 Nash, *Black Feminism Reimagined*, 13.
74 Mieli, *Towards a Gay Communism*, ch. 2.

75 The lyrics in this verse are a remnant from an aborted earlier song named "White Man."
76 DeLuca, "'I'm Not America's Nightmare.'"
77 Passen, "Welcome to Janelle Monáe's America."
78 Gwee, "The 9 Things We Learn."
79 See Vector 5: Postcapitalism for a more elaborate discussion of how this new social order is imagined throughout Monáe's work.
80 Muñoz, *Cruising Utopia*, 32.
81 Mieli, *Towards a Gay Communism*, ch. 5.
82 Penney, *After Queer Theory*, ch. 3.
83 Penney, ch. 1.
84 Yates-Richard, "'Hell You Talmbout,'" 45.
85 Collins, *Intersectionality as Critical Social Theory*, 44.
86 Hardt and Negri, *Empire*, 62.
87 Dardot and Laval, *The New Way of the World*, 3.
88 Foucault, *Power/Knowledge*, 59.
89 Villareal, "'Homecoming' Season 2's 'Pretty Gnarly' Ending, Explained."

Chapter 4   Vector 4: Posthumanism

1 Andrews, "Scarlett Johansson."
2 Doane, "Colorblindness," 15.
3 Brown, "From DelGuat to ScarJo," 16–18.
4 Shetley, "Performing the Inhuman," 13–19.
5 Byrnes, "Johansson's Real Performance," 29–35.
6 Lucas Hilderbrand's analysis is one of the very few published works of scholarship that has approached the film from this angle, seeing in the film an ambiguous acknowledgment of anti-Black racism, which hinges on the aforementioned scene in which the "revelation of a black body becomes the ultimate and absolute evidence of the character's non-humanity." See Hilderbrand, "On the Matter of Blackness."
7 *Her* (2013), *Ex Machina* (2014), *Lucy* (2014), *Westworld* (2016–present), *Blade Runner 2049* (2017), and *Ghost in the Shell* (2017) are all recent examples of this subgenre that somehow features Scarlett Johansson with improbable frequency.
8 Romano, "Janelle Monáe's Body of Work."
9 Roden, *Posthuman Life*, 9.
10 Hayles, *How We Became Posthuman*, 3.
11 Braidotti, *The Posthuman*, 46.
12 Jackson, *Becoming Human*, 46.
13 Braidotti, *Posthuman Knowledge*, 48.
14 McKittrick, *Dear Science*, 152–153.
15 Benjamin, *Race after Technology*, 36–37.
16 Chun, "Introduction: Race and/as Technology," 7–34.
17 Robert Walker, "The Sci-fi Saga of Cindi Mayweather & the Music of Janelle Monáe," *Nerd Reactor*, February 20, 2015, http://nerdreactor.com/2015/02/20/sci-fi-cindi-mayweather-janelle-monae/.
18 Replicant Roy Batty's abrupt decision to spare his hunter's life is among the most iconic scenes in science fiction film history, and his "time to die" speech among the most frequently quoted and sampled lines of dialogue.

19 Bukatman, *Terminal Identity*, 142.
20 Dutch actor Rutger Hauer is particularly striking as the Replicant's blue-eyed leader with bleached-blonde hair.
21 Chan, "Race in the Blade Runner Cycle," 73–74.
22 Braidotti, *The Posthuman*, 95.
23 Braidotti, 95.
24 Both narratives loosely adapt stories by Philip K. Dick, whose work has been a touchstone throughout Monáe's lyrics and music videos. For instance, the book title *Do Androids Dream of Electric Sheep?* (from which *Blade Runner* was adapted), is referenced on each of her concept albums, while the music video for "PrimeTime" is not only set in a nightclub called "Electric Sheep" but also largely replicates *Blade Runner*'s "neon-noir" aesthetic.
25 Perhaps coincidentally, Monáe has referred to herself as Alice in her lyrics. In "Django Jane," for instance, she raps the line "Wondaland, so my alias is Alice."
26 The original theatrical release provided a comically out of place "happy ending" in which no such revelation occurred and Deckard escaped the dystopian city with his Replicant girlfriend/sex toy beside him. The "Director's Cut" (1992) and "Final Cut" (2007) versions both end with Deckard finally understanding the fact that he is no different from the Replicants he has been hunting and killing, whereupon he grimly exits his apartment and slams the door behind him, as the screen cuts to black.
27 Jackson, *Becoming Human*, 3.
28 Jackson, 59.
29 Jackson, 11.
30 Jackson, 11.
31 Weheliye, *Habeas Viscus*, 27.
32 Yusoff, *A Billion Black Anthropocenes or None*, 76.
33 The Wachowski sisters' Matrix cycle has been a rare exception in this regard, representing the rebels as a majority-Black community, while the cybernetic Agents that pursue them are all too clearly the representatives of traditional heteronormative power: all are white men in business suits.
34 See Jeffords, *Hard Bodies*, and Tasker, *Spectacular Bodies*.
35 Matthews, "A Façade of Feminism," 9.
36 Mieli, *Towards a Gay Communism*, ch. 4.
37 Haraway, "A Manifesto for Cyborgs," 50–57.
38 Helen Hester, *Xenofeminism*.
39 Cuboniks, *The Xenofeminist Manifesto*, 55.
40 Cuboniks, 59.
41 A helpful contrast is offered by Kim Stanley Robinson's *2312* (2012). In this science fiction novel, many humans use technology to enhance their bodies toward a more fluid understanding of gender and sexuality. The storyworld also includes artificially intelligent humanoid robots who are described as almost unsettlingly androgynous in appearance, and who prove impossible to identify in terms of archaic gender roles.
42 Apple Music, "Janelle Monáe: What Is 'Dirty Computer'? | Apple Music," YouTube video, 2:56, April 25, 2018, https://www.youtube.com/watch?v=9w52Fhfgos8.
43 Atanasoski and Vora, *Surrogate Humanity*, 92.

44 See Finn, *What Algorithms Want.*
45 "Take a Byte."
46 Cuboniks, *The Xenofeminist Manifesto,* 59.
47 Braidotti, *Posthuman Knowledge,* 88–89.
48 Cuboniks, *The Xenofeminist Manifesto,* 55.
49 Hester, *Xenofeminism,* 64.
50 Hester, 65–66.
51 Weheliye, *Habeas Viscus,* 23.
52 Braidotti, *Posthuman Knowledge,* 41.
53 Weheliye, *Habeas Viscus,* 3.
54 Roth, "Disney Fascism," 18.
55 Atanasoski and Vora, *Surrogate Humanity,* 5.
56 Mbembe, *Necropolitics,* 158.
57 Jackson, *Becoming Human,* 11.
58 Derek Johnson, "Chicks with Bricks," 82.
59 Johnson, "A License to Diversify," 321.
60 Foster, "Tricks of the (Colorblind) Trade," 186.
61 Weheliye, *Habeas Viscus,* 72.
62 Atanasoski and Vora, *Surrogate Humanity,* 13.
63 Johnson, "Chicks with Bricks," 90.
64 Merskin, "Mia Had a Little Lamb," 285.
65 While later films in these franchises like *Toy Story 4* (2019) and *The LEGO™ Movie 2: The Second Part* (2019) tried to make amends for their predecessors' aggressively masculinist focus while also including more characters voiced by Black actors, the series' default anti-Blackness persists.
66 Kinane, "Janelle Monáe Shares the Beautiful Truth."
67 Rösing, *Pixar with Lacan,* 15–19.
68 Du Bois, *Darkwater,* 54.
69 Warner, "In the Time of Plastic Representation," 35.
70 Erigha, *The Hollywood Jim Crow,* 53.
71 Nash, *Black Feminism Reimagined,* 23.
72 Daniels, "John Boyega Is Doing What Star Wars Wouldn't."
73 Penney, *After Queer Theory,* ch. 4.
74 Warner, "In the Time of Plastic Representation," 34.
75 Camodeca, "Uncle Toy's Cabin," 59.
76 Camodeca, 52.
77 Douglass, Narrative of the Life of Frederick Douglass, ch. 1.
78 Marable, *Beyond Black and White,* "Introduction: The Prism of Race."
79 Jackson, *Becoming Human,* 33.
80 See Vector 1: Afrofuturism for a longer discussion of *Antebellum.*
81 Weheliye, *Habeas Viscus,* 90.
82 Weheliye, 110.
83 Atanasoski and Vora, *Surrogate Humanity,* 33.
84 Lorde, *Sister Outsider,* 31.
85 Muhammad, *The Condemnation of Blackness,* 15.
86 Nussbaum, "*Us* Movie Review."
87 Dyer, *White,* 44.
88 Jesson, "*Us* Movie Review."

89 Marcotte, "The Reagan Era and 'Us.'"
90 Edelman, *No Future*, 153–154.
91 Read, "You Will Not Replace Us."
92 Mbembe, *Necropolitics*, 78–83.
93 Mbembe, 74–75.
94 Mbembe, 92.
95 Jackson, *Becoming Human*, 71.
96 Jackson, 71.
97 Brown, *Black Utopias*, 172.
98 Brown, 112.
99 Mbembe, *Necropolitics*, 153.

Chapter 5 Vector 5: Postcapitalism

1 Taylor, *How We Get Free*, "Combahee River Collective Statement."
2 Szcześniak, "Blowing Glitter," 24.
3 McFarland, "It's Capitalism over Citizenship."
4 Desta, "Janelle Monáe: Artist in Residence."
5 Mbembe, *Necropolitics*, 177.
6 Penney, *After Queer Theory*, "Introduction."
7 Muñoz, *Cruising Utopia*, 32.
8 Jenkins, Peters-Lazaro, and Shresthova, "Popular Culture and the Civic Imagination," 11–17.
9 Bauder, "Why David Byrne Started Covering a Janelle Monae Song."
10 Grow, "The Last Word."
11 Wondaland Records, "Hell You Talmbout," 6:41, SoundCloud post, https://soundcloud.com/wondalandarts/hell-you-talmbout.
12 Redmond and Phillips, "The People Who Keep Going," 220.
13 Werner, *A Change Is Gonna Come*, 11.
14 Werner, 14.
15 Taylor, *From #BlackLivesMatter to Black Liberation*, 182–183.
16 Nash, *Black Feminism Reimagined*, 23.
17 Nash, 24.
18 Zacharek, "*David Byrne's American Utopia* Is a Grand and Glorious Plea."
19 Ivie, "*American Utopia*'s Chris Giarno on Movement."
20 Ferguson, *One-Dimensional Queer*, 21.
21 Ivie, "*American Utopia*'s Chris Giarno."
22 Jameson, *An American Utopia*, 31.
23 Dean, "Dual Power Redux," 110.
24 Robinson, *Cedric J. Robinson*, 152.
25 Jameson, *An American Utopia*, 20.
26 Toscano, "After October, Before February," 234.
27 Jameson, *Archaeologies of the Future*, 289.
28 Gilroy, *The Black Atlantic*, 43.
29 Arruzza, Bhattacharya, and Fraser, *Feminism for the 99%*, "A Manifesto."
30 Jemisin, "How Long 'Til Black Future Month?"
31 Hoffer, "Janelle Monáe's 'Many Moons.'"
32 Jackson, *Becoming Human*, 4.

33 Singh, *Race and America's Long War*, 179.
34 Zamalin, *Black Utopia*, 11–12.
35 Rieder, *Colonialism and the Emergence of Science Fiction*, 15.
36 Brown, *Black Utopias*, 8.
37 Gilroy, *The Black Atlantic*, 56–57.
38 Garforth, *Green Utopias*, 23.
39 Garforth, 12.
40 Monbiot, *Out of the Wreckage*, 6.
41 Streeck, *How Will Capitalism End?*
42 Miéville, "Introduction," in Thomas More, *Utopia*, 6.
43 Zamalin, *Black Utopia*, 144.
44 Brown, *Black Utopias*, 159.
45 Marable, *Beyond Black and White*, "Black Studies, Multiculturalism and the Future of American Education."
46 Robinson, *Black Marxism*, 307.
47 Robinson, 317.
48 Harvey, *The Condition of Postmodernity*, 147,
49 Roediger, *How Race Survived U.S. History*, 224.
50 Touré, "Sorry to Bother You: Is This the Most Shocking Anti-Capitalist Film Ever?"
51 Roediger, *How Race Survived U.S. History*, 68.
52 Ignatiev, *How the Irish Became White*.
53 Their voices in these sequences are dubbed by abrasively white actors David Cross, Patton Oswalt, and Lily James.
54 Singh, *Race and America's Long War*, 88.
55 Malcolm X, quoted in Taylor, *From #BlackLivesMatter to Black Liberation*, 197.
56 Yusoff, *A Billion Black Anthropocenes or None*, 73.
57 Arruzza, Bhattacharya, and Fraser, *Feminism for the 99%*, "A Manifesto."
58 Marable, *Beyond Black and White*, "The Political and Theoretical Context of the Changing Racial Terrain."
59 Gilbert, *Twenty-First Century Socialism*, 126.
60 Zamalin, *Black Utopia*, 17.
61 Wallace, *Invisibility Blues*, 216.
62 Horvat, *Poetry from the Future*.
63 Rindner, "Janelle Monáe Explains How Stevie Wonder."
64 Gilroy, *The Black Atlantic*, 37–38.
65 Horvat, *The Radicality of Love*, 119. Emphasis added.
66 Quoted in Horvat, *The Radicality of Love*, 109.
67 Smith, "Visions of Wondaland," 39.
68 Zamalin, *Black Utopia*, 16.
69 Olufemi, *Feminism, Interrupted*, ch. 9.
70 Brown, *Black Utopias*, 25.
71 Davis, "An Interview on the Futures of Black Radicalism," 243.
72 Quoted in Redmond and Phillips, "The People Who Keep on Going," 220.
73 Cedric J. Robinson, quoted in Camp and Heatherton, "The World We Want," 102–103.
74 "We live in capitalism. Its power seems inescapable. So did the divine right of kings. Any human power can be resisted and changed by human beings." Ursula K. Le Guin, quoted in Aschoff, "Ursula K. Le Guin, 1929–2018."

75 Ifeanyi, "Janelle Monáe fights COVID-19 Food Insecurity."
76 Horvat, *Poetry from the Future*, "Summer in Hamburg: Back to the Future."
77 Brockes, "Janelle Monáe: 'What Is a Revolution?'"
78 Baldwin originally spoke these oft-recycled words in a filmed debate with Kenneth Clark in 1963. Footage of this exchange was featured in the award-winning documentary *I Am Not Your Negro* (2016).
79 Gramsci, *Letters from Prison*, 300.
80 Taylor, *From #BlackLivesMatter to Black Liberation*, 163–168.
81 Osuna, "Class Suicide," 25.
82 James Baldwin quoted in Peck, "James Baldwin Was Right All Along."
83 Baldwin, *The Fire Next Time*, "Down at the Cross: Letter from a Region in my Mind."
84 Robinson, *Cedric J. Robinson*, 7.
85 Breihan, "Janelle Monáe—'Turntables.'"
86 In the midst of the global #BlackLivesMatter protests that erupted in the wake of George Floyd's murder, she posted a statement on social media that made an important distinction between her own role as an artist and ally, and the work being done by activists and community organizers: "I do not consider myself an activist or an organizer. I have a platform, YES, BUT there are people who ARE REALLY ABOUT THAT LIFE DAILY. I want to amplify their voices."
87 Toni Cade Bambara, quoted in Olufemi, *Feminism, Interrupted*, ch. 6.
88 Olufemi, ch. 6.
89 Monro, *Gender Politics*, ch. 7.
90 Muñoz, *Disidentifications*, 195.
91 Quan, "It's Hard to Stop Rebels That Time Travel," 91.

Bibliography

Abdurraqib, Hanif. *Go Ahead in the Rain: Notes to A Tribe Called Quest*. Austin: University of Texas Press, 2019.

——. *A Little Devil in America: Notes in Praise of Black Performance*. New York: Penguin Random House, 2021. Kobo.

Aceves, Rusty. "We Travel the Spaceways: Afrofuturism in Music." *SFJazz*, July 8, 2019. https://www.sfjazz.org/onthecorner/we-travel-space-ways-afrofuturism -music.

Aghoro, Nathalie. "Agency in the Afrofuturist Ontologies of Erykah Badu and Janelle Monáe." *Open Cultural Studies*, 2 (2018): 330–340. https://doi.org/10.1515/culture -2018-0030.

Ahmed, Sara. "A Phenomenology of Whiteness." *Feminist Theory* 8, no. 2 (2007): 149–168.

Allen, Joshua. "Why Organizers Are Fighting to Center Black Trans Lives Right Now." *Vox*, June 18, 2020. https://www.vox.com/first-person/2020/6/18/21295610 /george-floyd-protests-black-trans-lives-dominique-fells-riah-milton.

Amin, Takiyah Nur. "The Booty Don't Lie: Pleasure, Agency, and Resistance in Black Popular Dance." In *Are You Entertained? Black Popular Culture in the Twenty-First Century*, edited by Simone C. Drake and Dwan K. Henderson, 237–251. Durham: Duke University Press, 2020.

Andrews, Travis M. "Scarlett Johansson, Who Has a History of Casting Controversies, Says 'I Should Be Allowed to Play Any Person.'" *Washington Post*, July 14, 2019. https://www.washingtonpost.com/arts-entertainment/2019/07/14/scarlett -johannson-who-has-history-casting-controversies-says-i-should-be-allowed-play -any-person/.

Archer, Neil. *Twenty-First Century Hollywood: Rebooting the System*. New York: Wallflower, 2019.

Arruzza, Cinzia, Tithi Bhattacharya, and Nancy Fraser. *Feminism for the 99%: A Manifesto*. London: Verso Books, 2019. Kobo.

Aschoff, Nicole. "Ursula K. le Guin, 1929–2018." *Jacobin*, January 25, 2018. https:// jacobinmag.com/2018/01/ursula-k-le-guin-speculative-fiction-writer-books.

Atanasoski, Neda, and Kalinda Vora. *Surrogate Humanity: Race, Robots, and the Politics of Technological Futures*. Durham: Duke University Press, 2019.

Augé, Marc. *The Future*. Translated by John Howe. London: Verso Books, 2014.

Baldwin, James. *The Fire Next Time*. New York: Vintage Books, 1992. Kobo.

Bascomb, Lia T. "Freakifying History: Remixing Royalty." *African and Black Diaspora: An International Journal* 9, no. 1 (2016): 57–69.

Bauder, David. "Why David Byrne Started Covering a Janelle Monae Song." AP News, October 4, 2018. https://apnews.com/article/2f45dc6291fe4ca3b0520fe6a4150c97.

Benjamin, Jeff. "Janelle Monáe says 'Q.U.E.E.N.' Is for the 'Ostracized & Marginalized.'" Fuse, September 19, 2013. https://www.fuse.tv/videos/2013/09/janelle -monae-queen-interview.

Benjamin, Ruha. *Race after Technology: Abolitionist Tools for the New Jim Code*. Cambridge: Polity Press, 2019.

Berardi, Franco 'Bifo.' *After the Future*. Edited by Gary Genosko and Nicholas Thoburn. Edinburgh: AK Press, 2013.

Bertens, Laura M. F. "'Okay Ladies, Now Let's Get in Formation': Music Videos and the Construction of Cultural Memory." *Open Cultural Studies* 1, no. 1 (2017): 88–98. https://doi.org/10.1515/culture-2017-0009.

Bird, Joshua. "Climbing Aboard the Mothership: An Afrofuturistic Reading of Parliament-Funkadelic." *Occam's Razor*, 3 (2016): 29–33.

Bleznak, Becca. "Why Janelle Monáe Says 1 'I May Destroy You' Moment Brought Tears to her Eyes." Showbiz Cheatsheet, September 16, 2020. https://www.cheatsheet .com/entertainment/janella-monae-i-may-destroy-you-moment-tears-eyes.html/.

Bloch, Ernst. *The Principle of Hope*. Translated by Neville Plaice, Stephen Plaice, and Paul Knight. Cambridge: MIT Press, 1995.

Bonneuil, Christophe, and Jean-Baptiste Fressoz. *The Shock of the Anthropocene: The Earth, History, and Us*. Translated by David Fernbach. London: Verso Books, 2016.

Bould, Mark. "The Ships Landed Long Ago: Afrofuturism and Black SF." *Science Fiction Studies* 34, no. 2 (2007): 177–186.

Bowrey, Kathy. "The New Intellectual Property: Celebrity, Fans and the Properties of the Entertainment Franchise." *Griffith Law Review* 20, no. 1 (2011): 188–220.

Braidotti, Rosi. *The Posthuman*. Cambridge: Polity Press, 2013.

———. *Posthuman Knowledge*. Cambridge: Polity Press, 2019.

Breihan, Tom. "Best New Track: Janelle Monáe, 'Tightrope' (ft. Big Boi)." *Pitchfork*, February 22, 2010. https://pitchfork.com/reviews/tracks/11790-tightrope-ft-big-boi/.

———. "Janelle Monáe—'Turntables.'" *Stereogum*, September 8, 2020. https://www .stereogum.com/2097334/janelle-monae-turntables/music/.

Brock, André Jr. *Distributed Blackness: African American Cybercultures*. New York: New York University Press, 2020.

Brockes, Emma. "Janelle Monáe: 'What Is a Revolution without a Song?'" *The Guardian*, September 26, 2020. https://www.theguardian.com/music/2020/sep/26 /janelle-monae-what-is-a-revolution-without-a-song.

Brooks, Daphne A. *Liner Notes for the Revolution: The Intellectual Life of Black Feminist Sound*. Cambridge: The Belknap Press of Harvard University Press, 2021.

Brown, Adrienne. "New Formation: Janelle Monáe's Radical Emotion Pictures." *Los Angeles Review of Books*, May 28, 2018. https://lareviewofbooks.org/article/new -formation-janelle-monaes-radical-emotion-pictures/.

Brown, Jayna. *Black Utopias: Speculative Life and the Music of Other Worlds*. Durham: Duke University Press, 2021.

Brown, William. "From DelGuat to ScarJo." In *The Palgrave Handbook of Posthumanism in Film and Television*. Edited by Michael Hauskeller et al., 11–18. London: Palgrave Macmillan, 2015.

Bryant, Taylor. "Janelle Monáe Is 'Young, Black, Wild, and Free' in Futuristic Music Video." *Nylon*, December 12, 2018. https://www.nylon.com/janelle-monae-crazy -classic-life-video.

Bukatman, Scott. *Terminal Identity: The Virtual Subject in Post-modern Science Fiction*. Durham: Duke University Press, 1994.

Butler, Octavia E. *Kindred*. New York: Beacon Press, 2003 [1979].

Byrnes, Alicia. "Johansson's Real Performance: Documentary Style in Under the Skin." *Science Fiction Film and Television* 11, no. 1 (2018): 29–35.

Camodeca, Gina. "Uncle Toy's Cabin: The Politics of Ownership in Disney's 'Toy Story.'" *Studies in Popular Culture* 25, no. 2 (2002): 51–63.

Camp, Jordan T. and Christina Heatherton. "The World We Want: An Interview with Cedric and Elizabeth Robinson." In *Futures of Black Radicalism*, edited by Gaye Theresa Johnson and Alex Lubin, 97–110. London: Verso Books, 2017.

Canavan, Gerry. "The Limits of Black Panther's Afrofuturism." *Frieze*, February 27, 2018. https://frieze.com/article/limits-black-panthers-afrofuturism.

———. *Octavia E. Butler*. Chicago: University of Illinois Press, 2016.

Carrington, André M. *Speculative Blackness: The Future of Race in Science Fiction*. Minneapolis: University of Minnesota Press, 2016.

Chan, Edward K. "Race in the Blade Runner Cycle and Demographic Dystopia." *Science Fiction Film and Television* 13, no. 1 (2020): 59–76.

Chu, Andrea Long. *Females*. London: Verso Books, 2019. Kobo.

Chun, Wendy Hui Kyong. "Introduction: Race and/as Technology; or, How to Do Things to Race." *Camera Obscura* 70, no. 1 (2009): 7–34.

Collins, K. Austin. "'Antebellum' Is a Revenge Fantasy Gone Sideways." *Rolling Stone*, September 16, 2020. https://www.rollingstone.com/movies/movie-reviews /antebellum-janelle-monae-review-1058960/.

Collins, Patricia Hill. *Black Feminist Thought: Knowledge, Consciousness, and the Politics of Empowerment*. New York: Routledge, 2000.

———. *Intersectionality as Critical Social Theory*. Durham: Duke University Press, 2019.

Cozzarelli, Tatiana, and Ezra Brain. "'We're Americans': Class and the State in Jordan Peele's 'Us.'" *Left Voice*, April 25, 2019. https://www.leftvoice.org/were-americans -class-and-the-state-in-jordan-peeles-us.

Crary, Jonathan. *24/7: Late Capitalism and the Ends of Sleep*. London: Verso Books, 2013.

Crenshaw, Kimberlé. "Mapping the Margins: Intersectionality, Identity Politics, and Violence against Women of Color." *Stanford Law Review* 43, no. 6 (July 1991): 1241–1299.

Cuboniks, Laboria. *The Xenofeminist Manifesto*. London: Verso Books, 2019.

Daniels, Robert. "*Antebellum* is 2020's worst movie, and an aggravating waste of Janelle Monáe." Polygon, September 18, 2020. https://www.polygon.com/2020/8 /31/21408649/antebellum-review-janelle-monae-horror-movie.

———. "John Boyega Is Doing What Star Wars Wouldn't." Polygon, June 30, 2020. https://www.polygon.com/2020/6/3/21278460/star-wars-john-boyega-black-lives-matter-finn-force-awakens-rise-of-skywalker.

Dardot, Pierre and Christian Laval. *The New Way of the World: On Neoliberal Society*. London: Verso, 2013.

David, Marlo. "Afrofuturism and Post-Soul Possibility in Black Popular Music." *African American Review* 41, no. 4 (2007): 695–707.

Davis, Angela Y. "An Interview on the Futures of Black Radicalism." In *Futures of Black Radicalism*. Edited by Gaye Theresa Johnson and Alex Lubin, 241–250. London: Verso Books, 2017.

———. *Women, Race & Class*. London: Penguin Classics, 2019 [1981].

Davis, Jonita. "How Black Women Are Reshaping Afrofuturism," *Yes!*, April 24, 2020. https://www.yesmagazine.org/social-justice/2020/04/24/how-black-women-are-reshaping-afrofuturism/.

Dean, Jodi. "Dual Power Redux." In *An American Utopia: Dual Power and the Universal Army*. Edited by Slavoj Žižek, 105–133. London: Verso Books, 2016.

Deleuze, Gilles. *Time and Repetition*. London: Bloomsbury, 2014 [1968].

Deleuze, Gilles, and Félix Guattari. *A Thousand Plateaus*. London: Continuum, 2004 [1987].

Delphy, Christine. *Separate and Dominate: Feminism and Racism after the War on Terror*. London: Verso Books, 2015.

DeLuca, Dan. "'I'm Not America's Nightmare, I'm the American dream': Janelle Monáe's New Kind of Protest Song." *Philadelphia Inquirer*, May 4, 2018. https://www.inquirer.com/philly/entertainment/music/janelle-monae-dirty-computer-20180504.html.

Dery, Mark. "Black to the Future: Interviews with Samuel R. Delany, Greg Tate, and Tricia Rose." In *Flame Wars: The Discourse of Cyberculture*, edited by Mark Dery. Durham: Duke University Press, 1994.

Desta, Yohana. "Janelle Monáe: Artist in Residence." *Vanity Fair*, May 19, 2020. https://www.vanityfair.com/hollywood/2020/05/janelle-monae-cover-story.

Dijck, José van. *The Culture of Connectivity*. New York: Oxford University Press, 2015.

Doane, Ashley "Woody." "Colorblindness: The Lens That Distorts." In *The Myth of Colorblindness: Race and Ethnicity in American Cinema*. Edited by Sarah E. Turner and Sarah Nilsen, 13–34. London: Palgrave Macmillan, 2019.

Donnelly, Ryan. *Justify My Love: Sex, Subversion, and Music Video*. London: Repeater Books, 2019. Kobo.

Douglass, Frederick. *Narrative of the Life of Frederick Douglass: An American Slave*. Fort Lee: D&G Media, 2019 [1845].

Du Bois, W.E.B. *Darkwater: Voices from Within the Veil*. London: Verso Books, 2016 [1920].

———. *The Souls of Black Folk*. Oxford: Oxford University Press, 2007 [1903].

Dyer, Richard. *White: Twentieth Anniversary Edition*. New York: Routledge, 2017.

Eagleton, Terry. *Hope without Optimism*. New Haven: Yale University Press, 2015.

Edelman, Lee. *No Future: Queer Theory and the Death Drive*. Durham: Duke University Press, 2004.

English, Daylanne K., and Alvin Kim. "Now We Want Our Funk Cut: Janelle Monáe's Neo-Afrofuturism." *American Studies* 52, no. 4 (2013): 217–230.

Erigha, Maryann. *The Hollywood Jim Crow: The Racial Politics of the Movie Industry.* New York: New York University Press, 2019.

Eshun, Kodwo. "Further Considerations on Afrofuturism." *CR: The New Centennial Review* 3, no. 2 (2003): 287–302.

———. *More Brilliant Than the Sun: Adventures in Sonic Fiction.* London: Quartet Books, 1998.

Fanon, Frantz. *Black Skin, White Masks.* New York: Grove Press, 2008 [1952].

Favreau, Alyssa. *The ArchAndroid (33 1/3).* New York: Bloomsbury, 2021.

Ferguson, Roderick A. *One-Dimensional Queer.* Cambridge: Polity Press, 2019.

Finn, Ed. *What Algorithms Want: Imagination in the Age of Computing.* Boston: The MIT Press, 2017.

Fisher, Lauren Alexis. "Janelle Monáe Delivered a Powerful Time's Up Speech at the Grammys." *Harper's Bazaar,* January 28, 2018, https://www.harpersbazaar.com /celebrity/latest/a15908951/janelle-monae-grammys-speech-2018/.

Forman, Bill. "Pop Sensation Janelle Monáe Uses Science Fiction to Convey Stark Realities." *Colorado Springs Indie,* June 10, 2010. https://www.csindy.com /coloradosprings/pop-sensation-janelle-monandaacutee-uses-science-fiction-to -convey-stark-realities/Content?oid=1739497.

Foster, John D. "Tricks of the (Colorblind) Trade: Hollywood's Preservation of White Supremacy in the Age of Obama." In *The Myth of Colorblindness: Race and Ethnicity in American Cinema,* edited by Sarah E. Turner and Sarah Nilsen, 173–191. London: Palgrave Macmillan, 2019.

Foucault, Michel. *Power/Knowledge: Selected Interviews and Other Writings 1972–1977.* Edited by Colin Gordon. New York: Pantheon Books, 1980.

Fraser, Wendy. *Fortunes of Feminism.* London: Verso Books, 2013.

Gainous, Jason, and Kevin M. Wagner. *Tweeting to Power: The Social Media Revolution in American Politics.* New York: Oxford University Press, 2014.

Garforth, Lisa. *Green Utopias: Environmental Hope Before and After Nature.* Cambridge: Polity Press, 2017.

Geffen, Sasha. "Janelle Monáe Steps into her Bisexual Lighting." *Vulture,* February 23, 2018. https://www.vulture.com/2018/02/janelle-mone-steps-into-her-bisexual -lighting.html.

Gilbert, Jeremy. *Anticapitalism and Culture: Radical Theory and Popular Politics.* London: Routledge, 2008.

———. *Twenty-First Century Socialism.* Cambridge: Polity Press, 2020.

Gilbert, Jeremy, and Ewan Pearson. *Discographies: Dance Music, Culture and the Politics of Sound.* New York: Routledge, 1999.

Gilroy, Paul. *The Black Atlantic: Modernity and Double Consciousness.* Cambridge: Harvard University Press, 1995.

Gramsci, Antonio. *Letters from Prison,* vol. 1. New York: Columbia University Press, 1994.

Gray, Jonathan. *Show Sold Separately: Promos, Spoilers, and Other Media Paratexts.* New York: New York University Press, 2010.

Grow, Kory. "The Last Word: David Byrne on Embracing Nonsense and Owning His Mistakes." *Rolling Stone,* October 21, 2020. https://www.rollingstone.com/music /music-features/david-byrne-last-word-interview-american-utopia-talking-heads -1077921/.

Gwee, Karen. "The 9 Things We Learn about Janelle Monáe in *Dirty Computer*." *W Magazine*, April 27, 2018. https://www.wmagazine.com/story/janelle-monae -dirty-computer/.

Haile, Rahawa. "Janelle Monáe, *Dirty Computer*." *Pitchfork*, May 1, 2018. https:// pitchfork.com/reviews/albums/janelle-monae-dirty-computer/.

Haraway, Donna. "A Manifesto for Cyborgs: Science, Technology, and Socialist Feminism in the 1980s." In *The Gendered Cyborg: A Reader*, edited by G. Kirkup, L. Janes, K. Woodward, and F. Hovenden, 50–57. London: Routledge, 2000.

———. *Staying with the Trouble: Making Kin in the Chthulucene*. Durham: Duke University Press, 2016.

Hardt, Michael, and Antonio Negri. *Empire*. Cambridge: Harvard University Press, 2000.

Hartman, Saidiya V. *Scenes of Subjection: Terror, Slavery, and Self-Making in Nineteenth-Century America*. New York: Oxford University Press, 1997.

Harvey, Colin. *Fantastic Transmedia: Narrative, Play and Memory across Science Fiction and Fantasy Storyworlds*. London: Palgrave Macmillan, 2015.

Harvey, David. *The Condition of Postmodernity*. Malden: Blackwell, 1990.

Hassler-Forest, Dan. *Janelle Monáe's* Dirty Computer. London: Palgrave Macmillan, 2022.

———. "'The Lion King' Is a Fascistic Story. No Remake Can Change That." *Washington Post*, July 10, 2019. https://www.washingtonpost.com/outlook/2019 /07/10/lion-king-is-fascistic-story-no-remake-can-change-that/.

———. *Science Fiction, Fantasy, and Politics: Transmedia World-Building beyond Capitalism*. London: Rowman and Littlefield International, 2016.

———. "Utopian Afrofuturism in *The Wiz*." *Science Fiction Film and Television* 9, no. 1 (2016): 88–90.

———. "Vision Quest of Fool's Gold: Looking for Utopia in Hollywood Science Fiction." In *Urban Utopias: Memory, Rights and Speculation*, edited by Barnita Bagchi, 235–256. Kolkata: Jadavpur University Press, 2020.

Hayles, N. Katherine. *How We Became Posthuman: Virtual Bodies in Cybernetics, Literature, and Informatics*. Chicago: University of Chicago Press, 1999.

Hester, Helen. *Xenofeminism*. Cambridge: Polity Press, 2018.

Hilderbrand, Lucas. "On the Matter of Blackness in *Under the Skin*." *Jump Cut: A Review of Contemporary Media*, 57 (Fall 2016). https://www.ejumpcut.org/archive /jc57.2016/-HilderbrandUnderSkin/index.html.

Himes, Geoffrey. "Janelle Monáe: Imagining Her Own Future." *Paste*, September 9, 2013. https://www.pastemagazine.com/music/janelle-mon-e/janelle-monae -imagining-her-own-future/.

Hoffer, Karlie. "Janelle Monáe's 'Many Moons': A History of Oppression." *Fandom*, January 28, 2013. https://genderlitutopiadystopia.fandom.com/wiki/Janelle _Monae%27s_%22Many_Moons%22:_A_History_of_Oppression.

hooks, bell. *Feminist Theory: From Margin to Center*, 2nd ed. London: Pluto Press, 2000.

Horvat, Srećko. *Poetry from the Future*. London: Penguin, 2020. Kobo.

———. *The Radicality of Love*. Cambridge: Polity Press, 2016.

Ifeanyi, K. C. "Janelle Monáe Fights COVID-19 Food Insecurity with #Wonda-Lunch." *Fast Company*, May 29, 2020. https://www.fastcompany.com/90510744 /janelle-monae-fights-covid-19-food-insecurity-with-wondalunch.

Ignatiev, Noel. *How the Irish Became White*. New York: Routledge Classics, 2009. Kobo.
———. "Without a Science of Navigation We Cannot Sail in Stormy Seas." In *Black Revolutionaries in the United States, Communist Interventions, Volume II*, 286–302. New York: Communist Research Cluster, 2016.

Irakoze, Judicaelle. "Why We Must Be Careful When Watching Beyoncé's 'Black Is King.'" *Essence*, August 1, 2020. https://www.essence.com/entertainment/only-essence/beyonces-black-is-king-criticism/.

Ivie, Devon. "American Utopia's Chris Giarno on Movement, Political Art, and Spike Lee's Lipstick Advice." *Vulture*, October 19,2020. https://www.vulture.com/2020/10/american-utopia-star-chris-giarmo-on-david-byrne-spike-lee.html.

Jackson, Zakiyyah Iman. *Becoming Human: Matter and Meaning in an Antiblack World*. New York: New York University Press, 2020.

Jameson, Fredric. *An America Utopia: Dual Power and the Universal Army*. London: Verso Books, 2016.
———. *Archaeologies of the Future: The Desire Called Utopia and Other Science Fictions*. London: Verso Books, 2005.

Jeffords, Susan. *Hard Bodies: Hollywood Masculinity in the Reagan Era*. New Brunswick: Rutgers University Press, 1993.

Jemisin, N. K. "How Long 'Til Black Future Month? The Toxins of Speculative Fiction, and the Antidote That Is Janelle Monáe." Blog post, September 30, 2013. http://nkjemisin.com/2013/09/how-long-til-black-future-month/.

Jenkins, Henry. *Convergence Culture: Where Old and New Media Collide*. New York: New York University Press, 2006.

Jenkins, Henry, Gabriel Peters-Lazaro, and Sangita Shresthova. "Popular Culture and the Civic Imagination." In *Popular Culture and the Civic Imagination: Case Studies of Creative Social Change*, edited by Henry Jenkins, Gabriel Peters-Lazaro, and Sangita Shresthova, 1–34. New York: New York University Press, 2020.

Jesson, Claire. "*Us* movie review." *Alternate Takes*, April 12, 2019. http://www.alternatetakes.co.uk/?2019,4,713.

Johnson, Derek. "Chicks with Bricks: Building Creativity across Industrial Design Cultures and Gendered Construction Play." In *LEGO Studies: Examining the Building Blocks of a Transmedial Phenomenon*, edited by Mark J. P. Wolf, 81–104. London: Routledge, 2014.
———. "A License to Diversify: Media Franchising and the Transformation of the 'Universal' LEGO Minifigure." In *Cultural Studies of LEGO: More Than Just Bricks*, edited by Rebecca C. Hains and Sharon R. Mazzarella, 321–344. London: Palgrave Macmillan, 2019.

Johnston, Maura. "Kesha and Dr. Luke: Everything You Need to Know to Understand the Case." *Rolling Stone*, February 22, 2016. https://www.rollingstone.com/music/music-news/kesha-and-dr-luke-everything-you-need-to-know-to-understand-the-case-106731/.

Jones, Cassandra L. "'Tryna Free Kansas City': The Revolutions of Janelle Monáe as Digital Griot." *Frontiers: A Journal of Women's Studies* 39, no. 1 (2018): 42–72.

Jones, Marcus. "Janelle Monáe's Radical Rebellion." *Entertainment Weekly*, September 15, 2020. https://ew.com/movies/janelle-monae-antebellum-digital-cover/.

Jung, E. Alex. "How Michaela Coel Wrote I May Destroy You's Dreamlike Ending." *Vulture*, August 24, 2020. https://www.vulture.com/2020/08/i-may-destroy-you-ending-explained-michaela-coel.html.

Kanigel, Rachele. *The Diversity Style Guide*. London: Wiley-Blackwell, 2019.

Kennedy, Gerrick D. "Commentary: On Its 40th Anniversary, a Look at How 'The Wiz' Forever Changed Black Culture." *L.A. Times*, October 24, 2018. https:// www.latimes.com/entertainment/music/la-et-ms-the-wiz-40-anniversary -20181024-story.html.

Kinane, Ruth. "Janelle Monáe Shares the Beautiful Truth behind *UglyDolls*." *Entertainment Weekly*, May 3, 2019. https://ew.com/movies/2019/05/03/janelle -monae-uglydolls-interview/.

Kooijman, Jaap. "The Boxed Aesthetic and Metanarratives of Stardom: Analyzing Music Videos on DVD Compilations." In *Music/Video: Histories, Aesthetics, Media*, edited by Gina Harley, Daniel Cookney, Kirsty Fairclough, and Michael Goddard, 231–243. New York: Bloomsbury, 2017.

Kreiss, Daniel. "Performing the Past to Claim the Future: Sun Ra and the Afro-Future Underground, 1954–1968." *African American Review* 45, no. 1–2 (2012): 197–203.

Lavender, Isiah III. *Afrofuturism Rising: The Literary Prehistory of a Movement*. Columbus: Ohio State University Press, 2019.

Leight, Elias. "Janelle Monae Talks Enlisting Brian Wilson for 'Dirty Computer' Album." *Rolling Stone*, April 27, 2018. https://www.rollingstone.com/music/music -news/janelle-monae-talks-enlisting-brian-wilson-for-dirty-computer-album-630328/.

Lester, Paul. "Janelle Monae. 'It's True. I Am Part-Android.'" *The Guardian*, April 2, 2014. http://www.theguardian.com/culture/2014/apr/02/janelle-monae-interview -david-bowie-prince.

Lorde, Audre. *Sister Outsider*. London: Penguin Classics, 2007 [1984].

Lordi, Emily J. "Black Radio: Robert Glasper, Esperanza Spalding, and Janelle Monáe." In *Are You Entertained? Black Popular Culture in the Twenty-First Century*, edited by Simone C. Drake and Dwan K. Henderson, 44–57. Durham: Duke University Press, 2020.

———. "'Calling All Stars': Janelle Monae's Black Feminist Futures." *The Feminist Wire*, September 25, 2013. https://thefeministwire.com/2013/09/calling-all-stars -janelle-monaes-black-feminist-futures/.

———. "Human After All: On Janelle Monáe in *Hidden Figures* and *Moonlight*." *Pitchfork*, January 12, 2017. https://pitchfork.com/thepitch/1408-human-after-all -on-janelle-monae-in-hidden-figures-and-moonlight/.

———. *The Meaning of Soul: Black Music and Resilience Since the 1960s*. Durham: Duke University Press, 2020.

Loreck, Janice, Whitney Monaghan, and Kirsten Stevens. "Stardom and SF: A Symposium on the SF Films of Scarlett Johansson." *Science Fiction Film and Television* 18, no. 1 (2018): 1–4.

Marable, Manning. *Beyond Black and White: From Civil Rights to Barack Obama*. London: Verso Books, 2016. Kobo.

Marcotte, Amanda. "The Reagan Era and 'Us': Sins of the '80s Still Haunt America in Jordan Peele's Horror Tale." *Salon*, March 23, 2019. https://www.salon.com/2019 /03/23/the-reagan-era-and-us-sins-of-the-80s-still-haunt-america-in-jordan-peeles -horror-tale/.

Matthews, Malcolm. "A Façade of Feminism: Scarlett Johansson and Miss Represen-tation." *Science Fiction Film and Television* 11, no. 1 (2018): 5–11.

Mbembe, Achille. *Necropolitics*. Durham: Duke University Press, 2019.

McFarland, Melanie. "'It's Capitalism over Citizenship': Janelle Monae on Our Dystopia Echoing Amazon's 'Homecoming.'" *Salon*, May 21, 2020. https://www .salon.com/2020/05/21/homecoming-janelle-monae-amazon/.

McKittrick, Katherine. *Dear Science and Other Stories*. Durham: Duke University Press, 2021.

Meikle, Kyle. *Adaptations in the Franchise Era: 2001–16*. London: Bloomsbury, 2019.

Merskin, Debra. "Mia Had a Little Lamb: Gender and Species Stereotypes in LEGO Sets." *Cultural Studies of LEGO: More than Just Bricks*, edited by Rebecca C. Hains and Sharon R. Mazzarella, 271–295. London: Palgrave Macmillan, 2019.

Mieli, Mario. *Towards a Gay Communism: Elements of a Homosexual Critique*. London: Pluto Press, 2018. Kobo.

Miéville, China. "Introduction." In Thomas More, *Utopia*. London: Verso Books, 2018.

Monáe, Janelle. "Django Jane: What Inspired This Song?" *Genius* 2018, https://genius .com/Janelle-monae-django-jane-lyrics.

Monbiot, George. *Out of the Wreckage: A New Politics for an Age of Crisis*. London: Verso Books, 2017.

Mondon, Aurelien, and Aaron Winter. *Reactionary Democracy: How Racism and the Populist Far Right Became Mainstream*. London: Verso Books, 2020.

Monro, Surya. *Gender Politics: Citizenship, Activism and Sexual Diversity*. London: Pluto Press, 2005. Kobo.

Morales, Wilson. "Exclusive: Janelle Monáe Talks Welcome to Marwen & Grammy Nomination." *Blackfilm*, December 19, 2018, https://www.blackfilm.com/read /2018/12/exclusive-janelle-monae-talks-welcome-to-marwen-grammy-nomination/.

Morgan, Joan. *She Begat This: 20 Years of the Miseducation of Lauryn Hill*. New York: Atria, 2018.

Muhammad, Khalil Gibran. *The Condemnation of Blackness: Race, Crime, and the Making of Modern Urban America*. Cambridge: Harvard University Press, 2019.

Mulvey, Laura. "Visual Pleasure and Narrative Cinema." *Screen* 16, no. 3 (1975): 6–18.

Muñoz, José Esteban. *Cruising Utopia: The Then and There of Queer Futurity*, 10th Anniversary Edition. New York: New York University Press, 2009.

———. *Disidentifications: Queers of Color and the Performance of Politics*. Minneapolis: University of Minnesota Press, 1999.

Murchison, Gayle. "Let's Flip It! Quare Emancipations: Black Queer Traditions, Afrofuturisms, Janelle Monáe to Labelle." *Women and Music: A Journal of Gender and Culture* 22 (2018): 79–90.

Nama, Adilifu. *Black Space: Imagining Race in Science Fiction*. Austin: University of Texas Press, 2008.

Nash, Jennifer C. *Black Feminism Reimagined: After Intersectionality*. Durham: Duke University Press, 2018.

Neiwert, David. *Alt-America: The Rise of the Radical Right in the Age of Trump*. London: Verso Books, 2019.

Nussbaum, Abigail. "*Us* Movie Review." *Asking the Wrong Questions*, March 25, 2019. http://wrongquestions.blogspot.com/2019/03/us.html.

Olufemi, Lola. *Feminism, Interrupted: Disrupting Power*. London: Pluto Press, 2020. Kobo.

Osuna, Steven. "Class Suicide: The Black Radical Tradition, Radical Scholarship, and the Neoliberal Turn." In *Futures of Black Radicalism*, edited by Gaye Theresa Johnson and Alex Lubin, 21–38. London: Verso Books, 2017.

Passen, Hana. "Welcome to Janelle Monáe's America." *New America*, May 10, 2018. https://www.newamerica.org/weekly/welcome-janelle-monaes-america/.

Peck, Raoul. "James Baldwin Was Right All Along." *The Atlantic*, July 3, 2020. https://www.theatlantic.com/culture/archive/2020/07/raoul-peck-james-baldwin-i-am-not-your-negro/613708/.

Penney, James. *After Queer Theory: The Limits of Sexual Politics*. London: Pluto Press, 2014. Kobo.

Quan, H.L.T. "'It's Hard to Stop Rebels That Time Travel': Democratic Living and the Radical Reimagining of Old Worlds." In *Futures of Black Radicalism*, edited by Gaye Theresa Johnson and Alex Lubin, 173–193. London: Verso Books, 2017.

Railton, Diane, and Paul Watson. *Music Video and the Politics of Representation*. Edinburgh: Edinburgh University Press, 2011.

Read, Jason. "You Will Not Replace Us: On Jordan Peele's Latest." *Unemployed Negativity*, March 23, 2019. http://www.unemployednegativity.com/2019/03/you-will-not-replace-us-on-jordan.html.

Redmond, Shana L. "This Safer Space: Janelle Monáe's 'Cold War.'" *Journal of Popular Music Studies* 23, no. 4 (2011): 393–411.

Redmond, Shana L., and Kwame M. Phillips. "The People Who Keep on Going: A Listening Party Vol. I." In *Futures of Black Radicalism*, edited by Gaye Theresa Johnson and Alex Lubin, 206–224. London: Verso Books, 2017.

Rieder, John. *Colonialism and the Emergence of Science Fiction*. Middletown: Wesleyan University Press, 2008.

———. *Science Fiction and the Mass Cultural Genre System*. Middletown: Wesleyan University Press, 2017.

Riley, Boots. "Audio Commentary." *Sorry To Bother You*. Blu-ray. Directed by Boots Riley. Los Angeles: 20th Century Fox Home Entertainment, 2018.

Rindner, Grant. "Janelle Monáe Explains How Stevie Wonder & Identity Expression Influenced 'Dirty Computer.'" *Genius*, July 22, 2018. https://genius.com/a/janelle-monae-explains-how-stevie-wonder-identity-expression-influenced-dirty-computer.

Ringen, Jonathan. "How Singer-Songwriter, Actress-Activist Janelle Monáe Gets So Much Done." *Fast Company*, November 19, 2018. https://www.fastcompany.com/90263428/how-singer-songwriter-actress-activist-janelle-monae-gets-so-much-done.

Robinson, Cedric J. *Black Marxism: The Making of the Black Radical Tradition*. Chapel Hill: University of North Carolina Press, 2000 [1983].

———. *Cedric J. Robinson: On Racial Capitalism, Black Internationalism, and Cultures of Resistance*. Edited by H.L.T. Quan. London: Pluto Press, 2019.

———. *Forgeries of Memory & Meaning: Blacks & the Regimes of Race in American Theater & Film Before World War II*. Chapel Hill: University of North Carolina Press, 2007.

Roden, David. *Posthuman Life: Philosophy at the Edge of the Human*. London: Routledge, 2015.

Roediger, David R. *Class, Race, and Marxism*. London: Verso Books, 2019.

———. *How Race Survived U.S. History: From Settlement and Slavery to the Eclipse of Post-Racialism*. London: Verso Books, 2019.

Romano, Aja. "Janelle Monáe's Body of Work Is a Masterpiece of Science Fiction." *Vox*, May 16, 2018. https://www.vox.com/2018/5/16/17318242/janelle-monae-science-fiction-influences-afrofuturism.

Rösing, Lilian Munk. *Pixar with Lacan: The Hysteric's Guide to Animation*. New York: Bloomsbury, 2016.

Roth, Matt. "Disney Fascism." *Jump Cut* 40 (1996): 15–20.

Royster, Francesca T. *Sounding Like a No-No: Queer Sounds & Eccentric Acts in the Post-Soul Era*. Ann Arbor: University of Michigan Press, 2013.

Russell, Legacy. *Glitch Feminism: A Manifesto*. London: Verso Books, 2020. Kobo.

Salter, Anastasia, and Bridget Blodgett. *Toxic Geek Masculinity in Media*. London: Palgrave Macmillan, 2017.

Setaro, Shawn. "Reckoning, Celebration, and Reclamation: Janelle Monáe Dissects 'Dirty Computer.'" *Complex*, October 29, 2018. https://www.complex.com/music/2018/10/janelle-monae-dissects-dirty-computer.

Sharpe, Christina. *In the Wake: On Blackness and Being*. Durham: Duke University Press, 2016.

Shaviro, Steven. *Digital Music Videos*. New Brunswick: Rutgers University Press, 2017.

———. *The Universe of Things: On Speculative Realism*. Minneapolis: University of Minnesota Press, 2014.

Shetley, Vernon. "Performing the Inhuman: Scarlett Johansson and SF Film." *Science Fiction Film and Television* 11, no. 1 (2018): 13–19.

Shetterly, Margot Lee. *Hidden Figures*. New York: William Morrow and Co., 2016.

Singh, Nikhil Pal. *Race and America's Long War*. Berkeley: University of California Press, 2017.

Smith, Izzy. "Intersectional Feminism Triumphs in 'Hidden Figures.'" *Cherwell*, March 30, 2017. https://cherwell.org/2017/03/30/intersectional-feminism-triumphs-in-hidden-figures/.

Smith, Marquita R. "Visions of Wondaland: On Janelle Monáe's Afrofuturistic Vision." In *Popular Music and the Politics of Hope: Queer and Feminist Interventions*, edited by Susan Fast and Craig Jennex, 31–47. London: Routledge, 2019.

Smith, Murray. "Altered States: Character and Emotional Response in the Cinema." *Cinema Journal* 33, no. 4 (1994): 34–56.

Spanos, Brittany. "Janelle Monáe Frees Herself." *Rolling Stone*, April 26, 2018. https://www.rollingstone.com/music/music-features/janelle-monae-frees-herself-629204/.

———. "Janelle Monáe Talks Writing Stacey Abrams Doc Theme: 'What Is a Revolution without a Song?'" *Rolling Stone*, September 15, 2020. https://www.rollingstone.com/music/music-news/janelle-monae-turntables-interview-1057188/.

Steinmetz, Katy. "The Transgender Tipping Point." *Time*, May 29, 2014. https://time.com/135480/transgender-tipping-point/.

Steinskog, Erik. *Afrofuturism and Black Sound Studies: Culture, Technology, and Things to Come*. London: Palgrave Macmillan, 2018.

———. "Michael Jackson and Afrofuturism: *HIStory*'s Adaptation of Past, Present and Future." In *The Politics of Adaptation: Media Convergence and Ideology*, edited by Dan Hassler-Forest and Pascal Nicklas, 126–140. London: Palgrave Macmillan, 2015.

Streeck, Wolfgang. *How Will Capitalism End?* London: Verso Books, 2016.

Suvin, Darko. *Metamorphoses of Science Fiction: On the Poetics and History of a Literary Genre*. Bern: Peter Lang, 2016.

Szcześniak, Magda. "Blowing Glitter through Straws. Revolutionary Moods in Lizzie Borden's 'Born in Flames' and Jill Godmilow's 'Far from Poland.'" *View. Theories*

and Practices of Visual Culture 26 (2020): 1–34. DOI: https://doi.org/10.36854
/widok/2020.26.2135.

Tasker, Yvonne. *Spectacular Bodies: Gender, Genre and the Action Cinema.* New York: Routledge, 1993.

Taylor, Keeanga-Yamahtta. *From #BlackLivesMatter to Black Liberation.* Chicago: Haymarket Books, 2016.

———, ed. *How We Get Free: Black Feminism and the Combahee River Collective.* Chicago: Haymarket Books, 2017.

Thomas, Ebony Elizabeth. *The Dark Fantastic: Race and the Imagination from Harry Potter to The Hunger Games.* New York: New York University Press, 2019.

Tolkien, J.R.R. "On Fairy-Stories." In *The Monsters & The Critics and Other Essays.* Edited by Christopher Tolkien, 109–162. London: Harper Collins, 1997 (1983).

Toscano, Alberto. "After October, Before February." In *An American Utopia: Dual Power and the Universal Army.* Edited by Slavoj Žižek, 211–241. London: Verso Books, 2016.

Touré. "Sorry to Bother You: Is This the Most Shocking Anti-capitalist Film Ever?" *The Guardian,* August 19, 2018. https://www.theguardian.com/film/2018/aug/19 /sorry-to-bother-you-is-this-the-most-anti-capitalist-film-ever.

Valnes, Matthew. "Janelle Monáe and Afro-Sonic Feminist Funk." *Journal of Popular Music Studies* 29, no. 3 (2017): https://doi.org/10.1111/jpms.12224.

Veen, Tobias C. van "Vessels of Transfer: Allegories of Afrofuturism in Jeff Mills and Janelle Monáe." *Dancecult: Journal of Electronic Dance Music* 5, no. 2 (2013): 1–41. DOI 10.12801/1947-5403.2013.05.02.02.

Verghese, Namrata. "Absent Center: Netflix's 'Dark' and Time Travel as White Privilege." *Los Angeles Review of Books,* September 7, 2020. https://lareviewofbooks .org/article/absent-center-netflixs-dark-time-travel-white-privilege/.

Vernallis, Carol. *Experiencing Music Video: Aesthetics and Cultural Context.* New York: Columbia University Press, 2004.

———. *Unruly Media: YouTube, Music Video, and the New Digital Cinema.* New York: Oxford University Press, 2013.

Villareal, Yvonne. "'Homecoming' Season 2's 'Pretty Gnarly' Ending, Explained." *Los Angeles Times,* May 22, 2020. https://www.latimes.com/entertainment-arts/story /2020-05-22/homecoming-amazon-prime-season-2-ending-explained.

Walker, Robert. "The Sci-fi Saga of Cindi Mayweather & the Music of Janelle Monáe." *Nerd Reactor,* February 20, 2015. http://nerdreactor.com/2015/02/20/sci-fi-cindi -mayweather-janelle-monae/.

Wallace, Michele. *Black Macho and the Myth of the Superwoman.* London: Verso Books, 2015 [1978].

———. *Invisibility Blues: From Pop to Theory.* London: Verso Books, 2016.

Warner, Kristen. "In the Time of Plastic Representation." *Film Quarterly* 71, no. 2 (2017): 32–37.

Weheliye, Alexander G. *Habeas Viscus: Racializing Assemblages, Biopolitics, and Black Feminist Theories of the Human.* Durham: Duke University Press, 2014.

Wekker, Gloria. *White Innocence: Paradoxes of Colonialism and Race.* Durham: Duke University Press, 2016.

Werner, Craig. *A Change Is Gonna Come: Music, Race & the Soul of America.* Edinburgh: Canongate Books, 2002.

White, Abbey. "Hidden Figures Has Inspired a State Department Exchange Program to Promote Women in STEM." *Vox,* August 11, 2017. https://www.vox.com

/identities/2017/8/11/16126144/hidden-figures-us-state-department-program
-women-stem.

Whitehead, Colson. *The Underground Railroad*. New York: Doubleday, 2016.

———. *Zone One*. New York: Doubleday, 2011.

Wilkinson, Alissa. "Why *Sorry to Bother You* Director Boots Riley Thinks Artists Should Be Activists." *Vox*, July 6, 2018. https://www.vox.com/summer-movies/2018 /7/6/17501500/boots-riley-interview-sorry-to-bother-you-coup-michel-gondry -activism.

Wolf, Mark J. P. *Building Imaginary Worlds: The Theory and History of Subcreation*. London: Routledge, 2012.

Womack, Ytasha L. *Afrofuturism: The World of Black Sci-Fi and Fantasy Culture*. Chicago: Lawrence Hill Books, 2015.

Wortham, Jenna. "How Janelle Monáe Found Her Voice." *New York Times Magazine*, April 19, 2018. https://www.nytimes.com/2018/04/19/magazine/how-janelle -monae-found-her-voice.html.

Wright, Julie Lobalzo. "The Boy Kept Swinging: David Bowie, Music Video, and the Star Image." In *Music/Video: Histories, Aesthetics, Media*, edited by Gina Harley, Daniel Cookney, Kirsty Fairclough, and Michael Goddard, 67–90. New York: Bloomsbury, 2017.

Yates-Richard, Meina. "'Hell You Talmbout': Janelle Monáe's Black Cyberfeminist Sonic Aesthetics." *Feminist Review* 127 (2021): 35–51.

Yuen, Nancy Wang. *Reel Inequality: Hollywood Actors and Racism*. New Brunswick: Rutgers University Press, 2018.

Yusoff, Kathryn. *A Billion Black Anthropocenes or None*. Minneapolis: Minnesota University Press, 2018.

Zacharek, Stephanie. "*David Byrne's American Utopia* Is a Grand and Glorious Plea for Human Connection." *Time*, October 16, 2020. https://time.com/5900617 /david-byrnes-american-utopia-review/.

Zamalin, Alex. *Black Utopia: The History of an Idea from Black Nationalism to Afrofuturism*. New York: Columbia University Press, 2019.

Zuberi, Nabeel. "The Transmolecularization of [Black] Folk: Space Is the Place, Sun Ra and Afrofuturism." In *Off the Planet: Music, Sound and Science Fiction Cinema*, edited by Philip Hayward, 991–996. Bloomington: Indiana University Press, 2004.

Media

Apple Music. "Janelle Monáe: What Is 'Dirty Computer'? | Apple Music." YouTube video, 2:56. April 25, 2018. https://www.youtube.com/watch?v=9w52Fhfgos8.

Donoho, Andrew, and Chuck Lightning, dirs. *Janelle Monáe: Dirty Computer*. 2018; YouTube: https://youtu.be/jdH2Sy-BlNE.

Horton, Peter. *Electric Dreams*. Season 1, episode 2, "Autofac." Written by Travis Beacham and Philip K. Dick. Featuring Janelle Monáe, Juno Temple, and David Lyons. Aired January 12, 2018, on Amazon Prime. https://www.amazon.com /Philip-K-Dicks-Electric-Dreams/dp/B075NTXMN9.

Lionsgate Movies. "Antebellum (2020 Movie) Official Teaser—Janelle Monáe." YouTube video, 0:59. November 21, 2019. https://www.youtube.com/watch?v =mXcZ7WDsVwk.

Monáe, Janelle. The ArchAndroid. Bad Boy Records/Wondaland 7567-89898-3, 2010, compact disc.

———. Dirty Computer. Bad Boy Records 7567-86579-3, 2018, compact disc.

———. The Electric Lady. Bad Boy Records/Wondaland 536210-2, 2013, compact disc.

———. "Janelle Monáe—Cold War [Official Music Video]." YouTube video, 3:43. August 5, 2010. https://www.youtube.com/watch?v=lqmORiHNtN4.

———. "Janelle Monáe—Django Jane [Official Music Video]." YouTube video, 3:16. February 22, 2018. https://www.youtube.com/watch=mTjQq5rMlEY.

———. "Janelle Monáe—PYNK [Official Music Video]," YouTube video, 4:28. April 10, 2018. https://www.youtube.com/watch?v=PaYvlVRBEc.

———. "Janelle Monáe—Q.U.E.E.N. feat. Erykah Badu [Official Video]," YouTubevideo, 6:04, posted by "Janelle Monáe," May 2, 2013, https://www.youtube.com/watch?v=tEddixS-UoU.

———. "Janelle Monáe—Tightrope [feat. Big Boi] (Video)." YouTube video, 5:12. April 1, 2010. https://www.youtube.com/watch?v

———. "Janelle Monáe—Turntables [Emotion Picture]." YouTube video, 3:05. September 15, 2020. https://www.youtube.com/watch?v=8CFrCk6orM.

———. Metropolis: The Chase Suite—Special Edition. Bad Boy Records/Wondaland 7567-89932-8, 2008, compact disc.

Various artists. Wondaland Presents: The Eephus. Epic/Wondaland 88875087262, 2015, compact disc.

Wondaland Records. "Hell You Talmbout." SoundCloud post, 6:41. https://soundcloud.com/wondalandarts/hell-you-talmbout.

Index

About the Author

DAN HASSLER-FOREST is an assistant professor of media studies at Utrecht University. He is the author of *Capitalist Superheroes: Caped Crusaders in the Neoliberal Age* (2012), *Science Fiction, Fantasy, and Politics: Transmedia World-building beyond Capitalism* (2016), and *Janelle Monáe's* Dirty Computer (2022).